Janet

Cornflakes and Candlelight

Janet Brady

Williams Publications

A CIP catalogue record for this book is available from the British
Library.

ISBN   0-9548598-2-0
          978-0-9548598-2-4

Printed in England by IntypeLibra,Wimbledon. SW19 4HE

Marketing and Sales
Williams Publications
8 Ranulph Way
Hatfield Peverel
Essex CM3 2RN
Tel:01245 381064

Some experiences continue to haunt us long after we have endeavoured to consign them to the past. One particular period needed to be threaded into a story so that I could be freed to get on with living.

JW

ALSO BY JANET WADE

The Angel Within

Safe as Houses

CORNFLAKES AND CANDLELIGHT

CHAPTER ONE

It was the greatest leap of faith I have ever made. I wasn't called upon to do it; it wasn't something that was required of me. Quite the reverse in fact. I did it because I was totally incapable of the alternative. I put down the phone, stricken by the enormity of the gamble I had taken with someone else's life. "She's coming home." I heard myself saying. "The day after tomorrow."

Events that had led to today's decision had begun, and staggered forward and back intermittently with each new change in Social Services policy, over seventeen years ago when Minty, clutching my hand beside her father's grave whispered, 'Now there's only you and me left at Three Farthings Mum. That's not very many is it? But I like you and me. We have nice days. You won't die as well will you? Promise.'

And I had given her the false assurance she sought because it was her greatest need and because I simply hadn't the courage to do otherwise. Musing on the challenges she had thrown me over the years, from finding a mate to making her famous, I decided this was surely the epitome. I must live to be a hundred. Well, if willpower had anything to do with it there would be no problem.

Minty has Down's syndrome and has been with me since her birth in a tiny town in northern Ontario, Canada, forty-five years ago. And thus I can claim without reservation to know her better than anyone; her passions, her fears, her likely reactions to all kinds of people and situations. I know when a 'yes' means yes, as distinct from the 'yes' she thought was hoped for or expected, or one that meant she didn't want to trouble anyone. I know what will herald joy or trigger despair; what will cause her to be anxious or confident. Not through any superior knowledge but because for over two thirds of my own life I have lived her life with her, and in doing so, recognise that I receive from her a love that is so special, so wholesome, that it transcends any other love I have experienced or imagined. Love that is absolutely unconditional, unwavering and unguarded. It is as if her need, and simultaneously her giving, has created a bond that on days like the one on which I made the decision that jangled bureaucratic nerves, is tangible.

And though so unexpectedly, we have had such fun together, not least generated by her unique language. Compared to Minty, Mrs. Malaprop was an amateur! I recall her telephoning her grandmother one day to tell her that we were going to a special concert, - 'the sort Mum loves Nan, to hear three famous opera singers.'
Teasing, to catch her out, Nan asked her who these famous people were.

"I know, I know," she had replied excitedly, and with a determination to impress, pronounced with careful deliberation, "POPPIOTTI, PLASTIC DINGO and CARELESS"!! Needless to say no one in the family has referred to Pavorotti, Placido Domingo or Carreras by their correct names ever since.

Over the years the thought would regularly surface that with only one parent she was vulnerable. I was sure that in an emergency her brothers would not fail to respond to her need, but they were married now with young families of their own. And if there was one subject my husband and I had always agreed on, it was that we didn't want our boys' lives to be limited by the responsibility for a handicapped sister. We loved them too much; had recognised how much of their childhood they had already given to someone they adored simply because she was there when they were born.
How difficult it must have been for them as later they coped with schoolboy taunts and curiosity about their sister who was patently different from other sisters. No one could be more compliant, cooperative, or eager to please, but her disability was visible nonetheless.
There was no disguising she was handicapped.

Moreover, it wouldn't be the boys on whom responsibility for her day to day care would fall, but on their wives. And however compassionate as people, they were not blood relations from whom such care should be presumed. It would be a wholly unjust burden to place on them, not to mention their own children who may have no problem with a handicapped aunt in their early years, but might find her, however fond they had become of her by then, an embarrassment as they became teenagers. Minty would not always be as capable as she was today, but would age prematurely and show signs of senility; might become incontinent, physically less well, and therefore more demanding of attention at a time when they could indulge their own social lives.

We had promised each other; a promise that had been reiterated several times when my husband knew he was dying, and one that I would keep. But increasing familiarity with 'the system' suggested it wasn't going to be easy, given not only my refusal, but sheer inability to accept anything less than the best for her.

No minor consideration was the potential link between Down's and Alzheimer's, and whether or not there was already a connection - for it is only with hindsight we could be sure - chatting to imaginary people became an evident characteristic in her early forties. These were mainly actors from the TV soaps she loved, for were they not her closest friends whom she saw several times a week and in whose lives she was so immersed?

Immediately after a programme she would have in depth conversations with those who had decisions to make or problems to solve, readily offering them the benefit of her advice. As yet the conversations were two-way and logical. She would assume the role of the character, and then her own in turn, which surely was not indicative of a degenerating brain so much as a longing for their company. But I was determined to keep her in touch with reality too, and as we had frequent visitors, this was not difficult.

A watershed had been reached around her fifteenth birthday, when I finally accepted it would be healthier if I stopped fighting what couldn't be beaten, and switched the emphasis from helping her to recognise letters and simple words - something she found so bewildering complex - to developing her social skills, wherein lay her interest. She so wanted to be part of a conversational group, to put visitors at their ease and make them so welcome they were reluctant to leave. She was never going to achieve in the academic sense so why put her through the struggle of futile endeavour; a struggle made even more daunting by limited eyesight. Better to nurture that which could be developed for her own fulfilment and to come to terms with the fact that there were limits to her potential. And set against our daughter's handicap, there was a whole family to be considered.

In age, her brothers were close on her heels and must be given the lion's share of help and encouragement in the academic field as they prepared for O Levels. With both of us working, it was a testing time, but fortunately our attributes were conveniently split. My husband untiringly coached the maths and the sciences, whilst essays and research for historical projects was the area in which I could help. The garden had to be put on hold - abandoned to be more precise. That must wait for distant retirement for there were more important demands on our time.

Despite the need to cram in so much into every hour, I felt more tranquil, having at last accepted that it wasn't possible to do everything for everybody. Our daughter's needs were significant because she was Downs, but no greater than those of her brothers who were now passing through puberty. Meeting needs had to be considered within the context of a family unit.

And so I ceased the soul-destroying attempt to help her compete with normality, accepting at last the restrictions that her handicap inflicted. Nonetheless she was a person in her own right, with her own strengths to develop. It all sounds so obvious now but in the quagmire of guilt, social conditioning, and necessity to conform - and prior to today's more enlightened attitude to mental disability - acceptance was, for many parents, a self-inflicted battle lasting years.

Often she would ask what to say to visitors, a situation she always initially found difficult due shyness, and we rehearsed a few pleasantries such as 'it's nice to meet you', 'do come again' etc.

4

"But if it wasn't nice or you don't want them to come again?" she persisted. With Minty there's only black and white; only truth and sincerity. I realised the futility of explaining that one says these things as a matter of courtesy, and how much easier it is when chemistry is there. And so we roll-played a few situations.

Next evening when she returned from her Centre, she stood in the doorway, and instead of rushing towards me with the usual hug, paused and then said, "I'll go out again Mum, and come back when you've remembered."
Mystified, I waited and the same thing happened. I followed her, kissed her cheek and suggested we have our usual 'coming home cuppa'.

"You've forgotten, haven't you?" she said seriously. "You're supposed to say, "Do come in. How lovely to see you!"
Which all goes to show how she can be neither tactful nor devious, nor would it be possible to teach her to be. She just straightforwardly reflects what she sees and feels, and it's best left that way. Just like the day we were in a queue of people being served somewhat grudgingly by an ill-natured shop assistant.

"Why is the lady being crabby?" I was asked, and I feared the lady herself must have heard.

"Maybe she's having a bad day or she's not feeling well," I whispered, putting my finger to my lips.
She said no more and we waited our turn. Purchase duly wrapped, we were given our change, and to my embarrassment Minty patted the assistant's hand.

"I expect you'll feel better this afternoon," she assured her. "Go and have a nice cup of tea."

Years later, when the boys had married, and my husband had died, I began the search to find a way to protect her future. Months of travelling, getting lost, finding off the beaten track addresses, culminated in the decision that if for any reason I could no longer care for her, then Home Farm Trust offered the best set of circumstances for her particular needs, with both educational and domestic facilities on site.

Our first visit is still imprinted on my memory. The Manager had shown us around, answered our questions and then suggested we stayed for lunch.

"It's my birthday," he said to Minty, "so the residents have planned something special in the dining room. Will you sit at my table and keep me company?"

He had instinctively sensed the best way to engage her, for birthdays, no matter whose, are special. Minty would rather walk into a group who spontaneously sang Happy Birthday to her than receive a dozen presents. She released my hand and took his. He picked up the beginning of trust and throughout lunch they could have been life-long buddies. He poured her a second glass of juice, refilled his own, and threw me a questioning glance as she registered concern.

"Be careful," she warned seriously. "You might get *brothelised*!!"

"Now that could be interesting," he declared. "Tempting even!"

Best leave on a high, and we thanked him and accepted his invitation to return. It was obviously too good an opportunity for him to miss, and he said casually, "I've enjoyed the laughs we've had. Come again near to your birthday and we'll have another special occasion. Maybe Mum could go and do some shopping. Stay overnight if you like. We sometimes have a spare room."

I could almost see the thoughts crossing her brow as she sought how to remain polite whilst not yet acceding. Knowing her as I do I guessed what her words would be even before she said them.

"I'm sorry you'll miss my laughs," she said earnestly, "but I've thought of a better idea. You come and have a birthday lunch with us and *you* stay overnight. Now we haven't got Dad and my brothers, we've got two spare rooms *all* the time!"

Grinning broadly, he gestured defeat. "Knocked out in the first round!" he whispered. "Jumping the fences too fast but she looked so confident I thought I could capitalise. And I tell you now, it would be an absolute joy to have her."

"And I would be giving you the greatest gift," I said, suddenly incapable of contemplating her absence. Why are such people in this world? And how do they evoke such love and protection? Totally vulnerable, they live as the proverbial lilies of the field, worrying not for the morrow but valuing the precious moments of today, wasting not a jot on envy, malice or greed; factors that in any case are not part of their makeup or comprehension.

He was a good man; we would return and take things very slowly, not only because the situation demanded it, but because I wanted to hang on to each precious day we had left together. We did exactly that until she became familiar and comfortable with the situation.

So proudly did the residents show off their housekeeping, and for those capable of taking a bus, there was a satellite home from which the residents could go to college or access the on site training. Minty wouldn't manage the former due such poor eyesight that she cannot safely cross a road or read a bus number, but each time we visited she talked of performing on Open Days, of sharing one of the tiny bungalows with a friend and inviting me over to tea under a parasol in her tiny garden.

She would make her own breakfast and simple sandwiches in the bungalow which was equipped with a microwave, electric kettle etc, and for her cooked meals would go to the delightful beamed dining room in the main house. There was a laundry, barns in which to learn how to weave and participate in arts and crafts, whilst the thriving drama club continued to hold most appeal for her. There were ponies to ride and people close by to help and direct, or to keep a distance as independence grew. The Manager's house was only yards from the bungalows in this secure, safe, traffic free environment in which, even with her limited eyesight, she could walk unaccompanied to her various activities. Here she could live a fulfilled life.

At twenty-seven she was ready and eager; the timing perfect. She would be doing what she most wanted - emulating her brothers who now had their own homes and independence. We were both becoming accustomed to the idea, and though I knew what heart wrenching lay ahead, how empty life would suddenly be without her, we were ready to give it our best shot.

"Go and talk to your local authority," a member of staff advised. "It's likely one of the bungalows will be available by the autumn."

My stomach lurched at the idea of such immediacy, but I kept the smile fixed. Minty really wanted this, and it was as near the perfect solution as we would ever find. So instead of going directly home, I visited local estate agents. The only way I was going to handle the fact of someone else taking care of her was to get a property in the area; somewhere she could visit if and when she wished.

* * *

But bureaucracy decreed otherwise. "We have our own county homes," one senior manager of Social Services asserted. "There's no way we would consider paying for Home Farm. Ours are perfectly good residences."

But I did not find them so. If I gave an arrogant impression they were not good enough for my girl, it was because they were not. She was far too precious to be given less than the best I could find, and over the years, the best featured only in the PR brochures, not the reality of Social Services budgets. In any case, the many we saw were literally 'Homes' from which she would be transported by mini-bus to the local training centre, or not, whilst Home Farm with training and educational facilities on sight could give her the degree of independence of which she was capable.

I set about doing a costing exercise and after some weeks of wheedling figures from reluctant clerks, I presented my findings. It would cost exactly eleven pounds a week more for her to be at Home Farm than for her to be in residence in any of the county homes offered, with the additional cost of transport to a training centre on weekdays.

"I will cover that eleven pounds as long as I'm alive," I promised. "And when I fall off my perch there will be a house to finance the surplus for as long as necessary. Now, will you agree to her going to Home Farm?"

But 'there was no machinery to enable such a financial arrangement,' I was informed.

"You mean it's beyond the wit of your department to organise?" I asked incredulously of one department head. He chose not to reply.

I would, I told him, be happy to bring a group of average ten year olds who would do the sums for him. Trying unsuccessfully to conceal his irritation, I was politely, if coolly, shown the door, and as it closed resolutely behind me, I sensed the indignation aroused by this wretched woman who had just wasted his time.

I was angry because I knew we were letting the best chance of her being able to adjust to another way of life, slip away. If we didn't seize the moment, leaving home would, as time passed, become nothing less than traumatic. If we were to do it, it must be soon.

I don't suppose he stopped to consider the state to which he had reduced me. I was after all just another statistic. I fumbled for my car keys and fought to pull myself together as I drove to a headteachers' meeting with education department personnel to be enlightened about new government requirements re 'Special Needs in Primary School'. No use trying to tell anyone without a handicapped child that legal requirements are light years from actually meeting them, or acting promptly on their recognition.

Parents of a special needs child will know. Only they, whilst fighting and waiting, will have been through the torment of watching people climb career ladders on the back of a new initiative distributed in glossy brochures, and who then don't stay around long enough to see it killed off by a departmental decision to spend the money on something with the potential to attract more votes.

From somewhere I must find the will to continue the search; well nigh impossible given that not only must we now relinquish the obvious best choice having searched so long to find it, but because deep down I had no wish to let her go anyway. I wanted to care for her as long as she needed me. It was so easy for other people to say 'You must find somewhere. You can't live forever. Better she goes whilst you are here to help her make the transition.....'

Did they think I didn't know I couldn't live forever? Or that I hadn't told myself a hundred times that I must plan for a future that may or may not happen? There isn't a day goes by without anguish that I may predecease her. It is my last thought at night, and my first each morning.

And yes of course what they said was sensible. But could they adopt the same plan with their child and hand over their seven year old, just in case they were killed in a road accident before she grew up? Because that's what she was; a child locked in an adult body. Still with a child's need of love and protection; still with a seven year old's expectation of parental care, provision of a home and all that that implies, no matter how political correctness decrees we should describe her.

She will never, despite government initiatives to label her so, be independent. She might be able to do the simplest of jobs - and does - for a couple of hours a week, but she needs an able body to drive her there, to check any relevant paperwork, to liase with staff in charge, and to bring her home again. The only truly reliable comment comes someone who has walked the same path. If he also happens to be an expert, then that is an almighty bonus.

I think often of a homily I came across whilst on an Indian reservation in Canada. 'Until you have worn my moccasins, don't criticise the tracks I have made.'

CHAPTER TWO

And then had come the literal body blow. Further symptoms after leaving hospital for minor surgery suggested a more serious concern, serious enough for our GP to have me in front of a consultant within twenty-four hours. My mind had trouble focussing as he responded to the question I struggled to articulate.
Straight from the shoulder he said, "50-50".

He didn't know then I had a handicapped daughter or that she had already lost her father to the big C. My fear, he told me afterwards, had been palpable. But he had mistaken the nature of it. It had not been a fear of surgery, or even dying itself. I could not die. It wasn't an option. I had someone to care for; someone I simply had to stay alive for. For over forty years I had thought for two people; she was as much a part of me as my own limbs and a darn sight more precious, for she is everything that is good and wholesome.

My life is structured around her needs, my coming and goings around her timetable. She has become my life to the point where I literally don't know where the parameters of her life begin and those of mine end. We have been on our own now for nearly twenty years so that living a double life without recourse to a partner is now the norm. She is half my existence. Not a neatly defined half that can be separated cleanly, but half the muddled mass that was me.

But the fear was over now and the consultant smiled reassuringly as I emerged from the anaesthetic. "I didn't find anything," he assured. "False alarm. All's well."
We could go on as normal, but I had been jolted into an awareness of my own mortality. Nowadays Downs people could live into their sixties. And Home Farm continued to be vetoed.

My buffer was knowing that if I died suddenly, my sister and brother in law would come and stay with Minty so that she would be spared losing her home, and me, simultaneously. I have always been grateful that they didn't wait to be asked, but insisted on being her godparents for that very reason, well knowing, and fully accepting what such a commitment would mean. They have never wavered in that commitment, and would also see to it that Minty could spend as much time abroad with her brothers and their families as was a pleasure for both them, and her.

It had not escaped my attention that though she idolised her brothers, she was less eager as the years progressed to spend time in a young family environment. She had begun to find children tiring, and before they were out of the drive after a visit, began the process of tidying toys, crayons and works of art. The premature ageing I had been warned of, was on the horizon. She wanted an ordered, uncomplicated and quiet life.

In an ideal world of course my sister would be much younger than I, not of my generation, but we must live with the world as it is, and not as we would have it. In almost every other instance a godparent assumes more than a passive interest if and when a child is unexpectedly orphaned, an involvement that lessens in intensity as he comes of age. The parents of a handicapped child for whom independent adulthood is barred, and for whom 'childhood' is a lifetime condition, must seek godparents with meticulous care, if indeed choice is available. And the godparents, however compassionate, must not agree to the responsibility without the most serious heart searching.

As the years passed, no matter the political colour, council belts were pulled ever more tightly. Increasingly they could provide, only in cases of most serious need. Wearied by the fight, I decided to put the problem on the back boiler until I was sixty. The more immediate problem was to continue to juxtapose our two lives. For all the years I had been widowed and held down a professional job to support the two of us, Minty's minibus had arrived before 8am, enabling me to get to my school by ten past, and to remain on site until after 5.30, knowing we'd then get home around the same time.

In those early days of Local Management of Schools, and the gradual transfer of power from local authority to individual boards of governors coinciding with the instigation of the National Curriculum, endless staff meetings and long hours were the norm, and my briefcase bulged each evening with documents to be read after Minty had gone to bed.

But now things were changing equally fast in Social Services - and adversely as far as we were concerned. Transport and indeed every aspect of care for the handicapped would be subjected to change and cutbacks as departments aspired to become 'leaner and fitter', and what was once dealt with cohesively under one umbrella, became fragmented and uncoordinated as departmental heads put contracts out to tender. Often pressured to accept the lowest bidders, it was discovered later that once contracts were won, corners were cut and standards dropped.

It was likely that in time, the hours Minty could spend at her Training Centre would be reduced, and transport would arrive later, and return earlier, as indeed proved to be the case. I had worked for a lifetime; maybe it would soon be time to call it a day. I informed the school chair that if, as seemed likely, I could no longer make the same 110% commitment, then this must be my last year.

Decision made, I was determined to leave everything shipshape and in full sail for my successor. But one day of the weekend was always for Minty and working around school fetes and fund raising events, football and netball matches, we planned an outing for either Saturday or Sunday, even if only an hour or so, for I was aware that her stamina was decreasing.

One summer afternoon at a medieval jousting display, I noticed she was tiring, and suggested refreshment in what had once been the baronial hall. Sitting together in those awesome surroundings, I explained that the castle had been here for over four hundred years, hence the decay. Minty sipped her tea thoughtfully, apparently unimpressed, and then declared innocently, "So that's why these scones are so hard. They've been here all that time!"

The search for 'a Home' was resumed, often two in a week, and then periodically I would limply set the whole issue aside, so frustrated by the lack of communication between departments and failure to return calls, and most of all by the continuous staff changes and absences, that I'd vent my frustration on a piece of writing and vow not to depend on outside agencies but somehow find a way to do it all myself. And to be honest, sometimes I'd be glad of the council's lack of communication, for that gave reason for us to stay together without feeling guilty about my lack of progress.

Literally at my wits end, exhausted by introspection and worry, and for a reason I cannot define to this day, I consulted a medium, telling her nothing of my circumstances. Previously sceptical of such notions, I wasn't looking for tall handsome strangers, money or fame, but for the assurance I wanted, despite my scepticism. But in a one sided conversation, - hers because I was determined to give her no lead, - she alluded to an independent streak stretching into 'old age.' Two words that were music to my ears. Justifiably or not, I was comforted for a long time with that 'information'; in fact acted on it, or rather became inactive, and stopped visiting Homes.

There was a period when I noticed a slight, but distinct loss of short-term memory in my daughter. I watched carefully and sought expert opinion for I didn't know what it might preface. Describing incidents and occurrences, it was suggested that we might be at the outset of Alzheimer's, though it wasn't possible to predict with any certainty. Indeed, I was told that only with hindsight could one be sure about the early stages. It came as a shock to be told that from beginning to end would probably be about three years, in which case there was no need to continue the search for a Home. If the span were to be so short, the days ahead would be so priceless there was no question of her going anywhere. We had exchanged one problem for another and I must adjust my thinking accordingly.

But three years passed, and she stayed on a plateau. In the evenings she continued to 'talk' with her favourite TV characters, giving no impression she actually thought they were there; rather that in their absence, to *pretend* they were was next best thing. She was doing what others do for a chosen profession; she was acting. But without an audience. And yet she declined when I urged her to have friends home more often. She had rarely gained motivation from her peers, preferring so called normal company, especially jocular males who would tease and joke with her as her brothers and father had done.

One of the most rewarding times of her life occurred when an actor, obviously on a 'rest' period, had offered his services on a weekly basis to do some drama coaching. As a result she lived for Thursdays and rehearsed tirelessly for the various parts she played in the 'Ten Minute Theatre' productions. She idolised this tall, charismatic young man who had so unexpectedly entered her life. He was the topic of conversation at every breakfast, seemed to come through the door with her each afternoon, and occupied her thoughts each evening. She would rehearse being angry, excited, concussed after a road accident, the recipient of a glittering prize, or becoming a veritable star. Anything to win his approbation.

In a few short weeks he had given a new dimension to her life, lifting it from the humdrum to one of promise and expectation. She fairly bubbled down the drive one day, singing her way into the kitchen. "Guess what Mum!"

"Give me a clue."

"You remember we went to see the show called Mack and Mabel?"

"I do. And we loved it."

"Well next week we're going to do the Three Witches from Mack and Beth! Will you help me make a cauldron?"

There was a lot of adlibbing, and some fairly loose presentations of the bard's works. When they aspired to Romeo and Juliet, and Romeo, calling earnestly from the garden forgot to move into the spotlight, an impatient Juliet brought the house down when she muttered from her balcony, 'For goodness sake, where's he gone this time?' before descending to look for him and promptly pushing him up the ladder with a hefty heave-ho to his backside.

Evidently what they hadn't been told – and maybe he hadn't made this clear to the college - was that the young man had not agreed a set period of time, but had offered his services only 'until something came up.' And one day on her return it was crystal clear that little short of disaster had struck.

"He's gone," she wept. "Didn't come at all."

"Perhaps he's got a cold," I soothed. "He'll probably be back next week."

"No. Gone away. Not coming ever again."

Obviously an opportunity had arisen, and he was unmindful of the effect his sudden departure would have on those whose lives had been unexpectedly made so much more colourful by his being there.

As with most who are similarly handicapped, Minty dislikes and is toppled by change, even when prepared for it. So for the status quo to be altered without warning was little short of devastating. Years on she still talks of him, so significant was his input in making a 'stage debut' a dreamed of possibility for his students. To tread the boards was, from the moment he entered their lives, the oft-stated ambition. And whilst their carers, and he, knew this was virtually impossible, he had given them hope, with the resulting energy and aspirations.

"Perhaps we would see him on television," I tried to comfort. That had been his metiér previously. He must have had an offer he couldn't refuse to abandon them so abruptly and without explanation or message.

So it was something of a shock to hear months later that 'he's working in MI5 Mum.' Indeed it had been the talk of the Centre that day. What a famous person they had all known – and that being the case he would surely be able to take time out to come and see them again. It was difficult to conceive of the gregarious theatrical character being a 'mole', but truth is after all stranger than fiction, and they were all in absolutely no doubt about it, even if less clear of the purpose of MI5.

I pondered the possibility of his acting career being a cover whilst engaged on a more nefarious activity, or maybe he had been a high flying university dropout who had decided his potential was best fulfilled elsewhere.

I was later to discover that an opportunity had indeed arisen, and in the absence of any theatre or television work, our actor friend,

16

with a pressing need to pay the mortgage, had felt obliged to take the only job then currently on offer. I caught sight of him putting on a creditable performance of enthusiasm whilst selling a bathroom suite, when I went to buy a drawer handle in *MFI!*

CHAPTER THREE

In retirement I picked up the phone many times to engage with those who might help in planning my daughter's future. I needed to know what was available, and who could best assist to ensure a quality of life for her. But it was like walking through treacle. Staff were constantly reshuffled, promoted, had their job descriptions and thus their titles changed, seemingly putting them beyond the reach of those who most needed to make contact. It proved impossible to see or speak to the same social worker for more than a few months, and with each one we repeated the same information for the essential filing system. Conscious of the need to put every available minute of each meeting to good use, it was no good insisting this information was already to hand; was in fact in a dozen individual files, somewhere in the system. No, we couldn't proceed until personal details were recorded - again!

The law was being obeyed to the letter, but did anyone actually *read* files, or better, use them to inform successors and interested parties, thereby facilitating progress and saving time and money by so doing? Nothing suggested to me that files were passed around or information shared, and I imagined that as each of their authors gained alternative employment, they were merely added to a mountain of paperwork that was ultimately too daunting to read, and was thus bundled and set aside until after the 'sell-by' date. A legal requirement had been complied with to provide yet another statistic to advertise the 'efficiency' of the service.

'Reorganisation' became the buzzword. 'Must accommodate new directives.' Reorganisation to create an illusion of progress whilst simultaneously producing confusion and apparent inefficiency, with the resulting now almost obligatory demoralised staff. Sick leave to follow.

Despite the current necessity to graduate in order to become a social worker, communication is a skill that appears at worst not to be on the curriculum, and at best not to have been sufficiently emphasised for it to be mastered. Ironic that in these days in which technology enables rapid, instantaneous question and answer, contact is superficial and ineffective. It has become cheap and little more than a tool with which to keep litigation at bay.

'I've got a hundred emails to reply to,' was a common cry. Computers, laptops, mobile phones. Every device under the sun to make communication easier than it had ever been, and yet there appeared to be no cohesion, no coordination, no apparent inter-departmental sharing of information. For the handicapped person needing guidance it was all so insecure, so tenuous, and worse, so frighteningly remote.

In the absence of effective help maybe we could defer arrangements for the future a bit longer? I had regular checkups and still felt in pretty good shape. For a reason I did not comprehend, her life had been entrusted to my keeping, and that being so, surely I would be granted the longevity to see it through. But such a philosophy required faith, and I wasn't at all certain I had enough. Periodically conscience would stab and I'd put another call through to Home Farm.

'You won't get anywhere now without an assessment,' I was told. 'Phone your local authority and insist on one. It's your legal right.' I could hear the shuffle of papers, and guessed the recipient of my call was looking at records.

"It's twelve years since I first discovered you," I said. "We came often then, but for a number of years I've just stayed in contact with you by phone. Our papers are probably at the bottom of a drawer!" I was surprised to hear her reply. "Don't worry. You've remained on our register. I have your details in front of me."

And so I persisted as advised. But it was plain there was a dearth of social workers and those who were there, I was told, at their wits end to fit everyone in. Maternity leave, holiday leave, sickness and stress leave explained the reason for getting no replies to letters and queries. Despite assurances that my calls would be passed on - 'sorry you have just missed her. She'll get back to you as soon as she comes into the office,' - no response was forthcoming. I was reluctant to leave the house in case I missed a vital promised call, but the phone remained silent. Set against more urgent cases, we were not important.

I must push, shout louder if that was the way to get a result. At last, by going to the top, it was finally agreed for someone to call from another area. But such dogged persistence comes at a price. Battle weary and with nerves tattered, I feared my endeavours would actually have the reverse effect of solving my problem in that such a frenetic bid for attention to Minty, who was approaching forty now, would surely put me into an early grave rather than ensure I outlived her, which was of course the ultimate objective.

Having been this way too many times I made it clear that if my visitor were not intending to stay in post, I was unwilling to repeat information already provided and which none appeared able to access. Apparently 'remaining in post' was laughable, for the caller had been 'loaned' from outside our county in the absence of local staff busy dealing with emergencies. So I settled for insisting that 'only if the process of assessment could actually begin was there any point in her calling.'

I had been intrigued in recent years that professionals purporting to be under such pressure could spend so long on a simple exercise and chat over coffee about extraneous issues as if by having entered us into the diary for the morning, overwork could be assumed. Perhaps it was all part of the 'getting to know you' syndrome - pick up as many clues about the applicant today in case there's a staff change before the next visit. How different from the times when people stayed in post for years, gaining reliable insight, and more importantly the trust of their patient or client that would form the foundation for continuing care.

We began to fill in the substantial bulk of paperwork the Social Worker withdrew from her briefcase; bulk that was deceiving given the very large print. With hindsight I should have asked for a promise that once completed, the written assessment would also result in action. Hindsight is a powerful tool.

And so the process continued over many months. Though I was never at ease with the bureaucracy, I grew to like the young woman, appreciating her informed approach. It seemed that it might be more productive if the situation were to be played from the carer's angle. I was well into my sixties, widowed, had been in hospital....no family near...pretty good case really. Whilst it felt dishonest, it said far more about the shortcomings of 'the system.' Evidently this was the only way I could hope to get any solution for my girl.

Forms reflecting my comments were eventually returned for any correction I wished to make - and there were many - giving me the distinct impression that notes were completed when memory of the day on which comments were exchanged was no longer fresh – possibly only hours prior to the next visit, presumably due fitting in other 'extras' like us. And all through the process I heard how stretched resources were; how slim was my chance of getting what I wanted for Minty; indeed how slim the chance of getting anything at all whilst I was still able to stand and breathe.

It seemed we had bred a society in which people who shout loudest gain most. Those who retain a respect for authority, and deal in a courteous manner are pushed aside and remain unnoticed whilst attention switches to those who might arouse publicity or rock the boat.

And in the face of handicapped people literally being left with no one to care for them, how could I reasonably insist on care for my daughter whilst I was still in comparatively good health. I would want *her* to be given priority care in an emergency – could I be so demanding as to deprive others in a worse, and infinitely more lonely and frightening situation? I certainly could not. Perhaps too easily - because by now that eagerness to try living away had passed, I accepted the verdict.

Years previously, Minty had been keen to be part of all she saw on offer at Home Farm. She wanted a place of her own; to taste independence. Now, she tended to cling more tightly to that which was familiar and secure. And I didn't know if I could rekindle her

21

ambition for I too was correspondingly less confident as government goalposts were not only moved, but slithered precariously from one end of the field to the other. Yet I ought to find somewhere..... But where? Social Services had apparently closed all doors.

"I'm sorry," my visitor said, and I felt her sentiment to be genuine, but you're really not a priority and as I've told you, we're only able to deal with those in crisis."

She shuffled the file, giving an impression of relief that she had met with a legal requirement, and that I must consider myself fortunate to have got this far. And no, Home Farm like everything else would likely be refused. But what a waste of a ten month period if it was known ahead that there could be no result from having conformed with a government directive that everyone had a right to an assessment? And how naïve of me to imagine otherwise!

And I recalled the numerous times I'd had to explain to parents of our pupils that whilst they had a right to *express a preference* for a certain school, they didn't actually have a right to *choose* one.

Deflated, I thought of all those mornings that could more honestly and productively have been allocated to those priority cases. And what a waste of taxpayers' money. Not her fault. She had been sent in response to my pressure to be assessed, and had done her job. My frustration began to show. "Just as an academic exercise, what would I have to do to get Social Services to act?" I asked.

The Social Worker, at this moment I suspect, hating the system of which she must be a part, haltingly endeavoured to frame her reply within a hypothetical set of circumstances. "It had been known for people to go to the office, threaten to leave the handicapped person there, insisting they couldn't cope..... or for instance if you locked the door when your daughter was due home, refused to let her in and she was found by a neighbour wandering the street.....then of course we would have to take action."
So that was crisis management!

"Of course, I know you could never contemplate such a thing......"

"Damn right I couldn't." Clinging to the last shred of self-control, I closed the door behind her.

The upside of this wretched situation meant we could stay together - a salve to my emotional, if not rational, thoughts. Events and time had progressed to a stage in which I was fighting to do something I had no wish to do because both Minty and our family must be protected in the future. And now a decision must be deferred, not because I'd been the one to prevaricate, but because 'the system' was offering no option.

But there could be no peace, for whether rational reason or emotion prevailed, anxiety about the future would not go away.

It was Minty who stopped the downward spiral. She put the kettle on, laid a tray with our best china, hugged as only she can, and said, "Do you know Mum, I've always loved you - best in the world - ever since the day I met you!"

She picks up clichés from her soaps, and proceeds to quote them with only a 50-50 chance of their being contextually accurate. She poured the tea, looked thoughtful, and then asked seriously, "So how long do you think I've known you then?"

I feigned deep concentration and replied, "Do you know, I think it must be the same number of years as your birthday."

"Um," she said seriously. "As long as that?" And then, "It's nearly your birthday," she said happily. "I've done something special."

I squeezed her hand, imagining yet another of my vases had been 'expertly hand painted' with nail varnish.

"Can't wait!" I said, knowing that at this point she would be unable to resist giving a clue.

"Something to do with flowers," she added, and then with concern, "And I haven't told you the secret, have I?"

"It's quite safe," I assured her, amused by my own accuracy.

And thus I was taken aback next morning by a loud knock on our porch door. It was early for visitors; Minty wasn't even up yet.

Our local florist, an amiable man who took that little extra care, stood before me, appropriately clutching a large bouquet.

"For you Madam," he smiled. "Happy Birthday."

"What a surprise – who on earth......?"

"Definitely for you," he grinned. "Now do you want the bad news?"

"You are the bearer of flowers *and* bad news?"

He continued smiling, and then seemed slightly embarrassed.

"You don't need to look too far from home," he laughed, indicating the label. "Would you like to read it before I go? It's probably better."

Intrigued, I did as he requested. "It's typed."

"That's because the message was dictated over the phone. It's a lovely message, one most people would give their right arm for."

On the little card were the words, 'To best Mum. You not worry. We stay at Three Farthings all the time til I be 100. Love you so much. Every day.'

Realising now what the 'bad news' was, I held out my hand. "The bill?"

"Sorry," he grinned sheepishly. "We thought you must have known about it. He explained that she had phoned and asked for flowers to 'cheer my Mum'. The girl in the office had asked how she intended to pay for them and the reply had been an uncompromising, 'With money of course! My piggy bank's on the kitchen top where Mum does the baking. It's a red one.'

Apparently, in some consternation she had been passed to the florist who knew her from the times we have ordered flowers for friends, and he had teasingly asked whether she had a credit card. No, but Mum had. He could ask me when he brought the flowers!

"I doubt the piggy bank would yield as much as you need," I laughed.

"I've kept it to the basic," he assured me. "I should have checked with you but she had me round her little finger.... was so insistent and ...

".. sounded as if she knew exactly what she was doing," I finished for him. "She does, but she has no understanding of figures or money. I'm more intrigued by how she managed to locate you. She certainly can't see the print in the phone book ...." And then I recalled how I had propped a reminder on the kitchen table to order flowers for a friend in hospital. Minty must have copied the number.

"Look let's forget it. She's such a lovely person........" the florist began. "I'm sorry..."

24

"For bringing me flowers! How often do you think that happens to an over-the-hill, grey haired oldie!"

I wrote out the cheque and he closed the door and immediately opened it again.

"What do I do if she phones in again next year?"

"Just tuck the invoice inside the flowers," I said. "Only don't be persuaded to treat me like a prima donna, because for sure if she sees a film about a leading lady whose dressing room is filled with cascades of white roses, she'll ask you to do the same!"

"Right y'are." He relaxed, and then, "Maybe by next year she'll have forgotten."

I shook my head. "Stopping her love when she has found a new avenue for expressing it, would be like resisting a tornado."

He paused and looked at me quizzically. "That's wonderful. I've never realised... there *are* plusses, aren't there?"

"Hundred of 'em," I assured him.

He left with the agreement that we'd stick to chrysanthemums even if he did get future requests for orchids and roses! He reached his van, turned, and made a thumbs-up sign before driving off.

"Did you get my flowers? Do you feel happy Mum? Didn't I do well!" she beamed as she came home.

"They make me feel like a star," I assured her. "Come on, we'll go to the teashop and I'll buy you a treat to say thank you."

She was in her coat in an instant. "Can I order from the waitress?"

"Why not! I think you're becoming expert at ordering."

Half an hour later she pretended to read from the small print of the menu, and told me that I could have a 'lattee which was milky, or black coffee which was really brown with no milk, or one with cream, or.....', and here she paused for effect, "or, a Happy Cheeno. I think you should have one of those."

"Can I afford it?" I joked.

"I'm going to pay for it," she informed me. "I've got lots of money – look." And with that she emptied a pile of small change onto the table and said, "But sometimes people like paper money best, don't they?"

"Better have this then in case."

She handed the note to the waitress and pocketed the change! "There I've paid for the coffee and now you can pay the tip," she said patting my hand. "That's fair isn't it?"

CHAPTER FOUR

The weeks and months passed, and Nan came to stay. My mother hadn't been for her annual visit for the past two years, not having felt up to the journey so I was surprised when, now even more frail, she had suddenly announced her wish to come for 'about a week.' We drove up to the Midlands to collect her and though the weather was tediously hot she insisted the journey was manageable.

We made good time, and after resting for an hour or so, yes, she most certainly did want to hear the male voice choir whose performances she had so enjoyed on past visits, and who would tonight be singing in aid of a new church roof at a village nearby. Sitting in her wheelchair at the end of a pew, she hummed happily to familiar tunes. Friends came to chat at the interval and she drank a glass of wine, relishing new company and conversation.

The following day we were invited out to lunch and again I kept a close eye for any sign of fatigue, but none was evident and it was only reluctantly that she agreed to leave mid afternoon. On Monday we prevailed upon her to spend quiet hours sitting in the garden and having lunch outside. Neighbours popped round giving her again the opportunity she loved to chat.

"Enjoying your stay?" one of them asked.

She lifted her face to the sunshine and uttered a word I had never heard her use before. "I'm so content," she replied. "So happy."

But 'a quiet spell' was only as long as we promised to go to the market next day in the nearby town. "There's something I want to do. In all my life I've never bought black lacy underwear." A mischievous smile played around her lips. "Tomorrow I'll buy myself the slip of a lifetime."

27

'Who at ninety was going to see it?' I longed to ask. But it was obvious she had set her heart on it. It never occurred to me she was tying up loose ends.

That evening my mother suddenly raised the subject of Minty's future, which surprised me, and I was immediately uncomfortable, for when the topic had been aired on only two occasions in the past, she had resisted any suggestion of her going into independent living accommodation, insisting no grandchild of hers should go into 'an institution'. But this evening she was less abrasive.

"I've watched a few programmes recently. I understand your problem," she conceded, "and I can see it's tearing you apart. It's hard - maybe you do have to give it a try – the pair of you. If it doesn't work she can come home. But don't let it break you." And then almost to herself, "I know I wouldn't hear of it before, but the places aren't like they were when I was young. And now my own daughter is an OAP and none of us can live forever."

Minty who went to her Centre on Tuesdays, would not be coming to the market, so at breakfast she and Nan joked and planned secrets that I was clearly meant to hear.

"Ask your Mum to arrange supper at a nice restaurant tonight," my mother stage-whispered. "My treat."
The driver of the mini-bus hooted as he approached the house.

"Nan wants to go out for a meal tonight," Minty urged as she ran out of the door. "I think she'd like the Ferryboat Inn, don't you? And when I come back I'm going to give Nan that windmill picture I painted. Oh I can't, can I? I gave it to you. I know, we'll raffle it and Nan can win it!"

"Off you go," I laughed. "Have a lovely day and we'll all get dressed up tonight." I smiled to myself. 'Black lacy underwear into the bargain.'

"Are you sure you're up to shopping?" I asked tentatively. "You wouldn't prefer a drive to the coast?"

"We'll do that tomorrow," my mother declared in a familiar tone that brooked no argument. "This morning we're going to spend my pension."

I must have registered some concern at her zeal 'to go early so we can get a real session in,' for she chuckled and said, "Good Lord girl I'm shopping from a wheelchair. You're the one who's doing the pushing!"

I phoned the restaurant before we left, though not without difficulty. It was the third time since Nan arrived that outgoing calls were a problem, so I contacted BT and explained that with a handicapped daughter and infirm ninety year old visiting, I must have a reliable phone.

Nan did indeed buy her black lace petticoat, though not without a deal of ribbing from the East End vendor whose teasing she was well able to counter. She found a top for Minty and an azalea for my garden and was impatient when I insisted on stopping for a coffee. "I've just noticed that wallpaper shop over by the Chemist's. My kitchen could do with a new look. We'll call in before we go home."

And she did. The fact of the wallpapers being on the second floor presented her with no problem. She told the young assistant the colour scheme she had in mind and had him running up and downstairs for a variety of samples. When I offered to collect some, she refused. "No, you'll bring me the ones you think I'll like. This young man might come up with something we hadn't thought of – a fresh approach."

When she had finally made her choice, Carl, as she was now addressing him, looked at her with an exaggerated expectation of the commission he was about to earn.

"Three rolls please." she said, and as his face fell in disbelief, added, "It's just a tiny place, you understand!"

I refused to enter another shop, insisting we were going home for lunch, after which she would have a long rest before going to the restaurant. She protested but I stood my ground and finally she agreed.

"That paper will really brighten my kitchen up. Oh I did enjoy this morning. Could have stayed longer you know if you hadn't wilted."
She enthused about her purchases until we were half way home and then became strangely quiet.

My instinct went into overdrive. "You alright?"

She smiled. "Really enjoyed myself. Lovely morning."

We drove past the Common and I glanced at her again. "Five minutes and we'll have the kettle on."

"That's nice." She put her hand on her chest.

"Got a pain?"

She nodded. "Just a twinge. Cup of tea'll be just the job."

Pulling into the drive I said, "Sit tight while I get your wheelchair from the boot."

"Don't bother with it. I'd rather get in." She was already opening the car door. "I can manage those few steps."

She took my arm and was soon settled on the kitchen chair. I moved to fill the kettle but suddenly becoming breathless, she was gesturing to me to get her nebuliser. Her pallor was changing. Rapidly I plugged in the little machine and attached the mask but she seemed unable to summon the necessary strength to draw breath. Supporting her with one arm I reached out for the phone with the other and dialled an ambulance. Thank goodness it functioned normally. An ambulance would be here within minutes.

"Really enjoyed today," she whispered and lifted her head to smile. "Always wanted some black lace. And the paper - kitchen'll look a real treat."

And then her head fell forward, and it was all over. The mother who had held me in her arms since before I could even remember, died in mine, and I had not said 'goodbye'. It somehow seemed the gravest offence and I trembled uncontrollably at the shock of her being so suddenly beyond my reach despite our physical closeness. I was clinging desperately to her body, but *she* wasn't there.

I dialled again in case she hadn't really gone. "Please hurry," I begged, " but I think it's too late."

The duty officer began to tell me what to do and I obeyed mechanically, unable to accept it was all to no avail.

"Are you still holding her?" the voice asked. "Right, let her slide gently to the floor." I did as instructed, all the time pleading with her, "Don't go. Don't leave us." Then the phone went dead again. For the next hour, ambulance personnel, police, our doctor, an apologetic telephone engineer and the vicar, all surrounded me in bewildering confusion.

Minty was coming down the drive so jauntily. "Hi Nan! Did you fix the restaurant Mum? Guess what I did today...." And then her voice trailed. She may be retarded but she is quicker than anyone I know to pick up on atmosphere. "Mum what's wrong? Where's Nan?" she asked, even before she had closed the door.

And I had to tell her that yet another hugely loved member of the family had left us. We clung to each other and said nothing, because the silence where Nan had been was saying it all for us. Finally her grip slackened and she said as if it had all just come together in her mind, "I don't like people dying. Don't you go."

* * *

The shock of Nan's death occurring while she was on holiday with us, impacted like a tornado. One week of the year and it had happened on my watch, whilst I was caring for her. I should not have taken her shopping; should have made her stay in the garden. Stunned, I gained no comfort from our GP's assurance that for Nan herself, it had been a Rolls Royce of a death, – dying with no wearying pain on a morning when she had had fun doing exactly what she'd requested.

"People often get a surge of energy just before the end," he consoled. "And if you had refused, she would have worn herself out persuading you."

"But she won't get to wear her black lace," I said stupidly, too distraught to notice whether he raised an eyebrow.

"Even better," he declared. "The best possible day for her with still something to look forward to for the evening." His answer didn't strike me as strange but instead robbed death of its finality.

Arrangements had to be made for her body be returned to the Midlands where she was to be buried with my father, and in the following days my girl stuck like a shadow, and yet seemed less distressed.

31

"I've worked it all out," she said quite suddenly over coffee. "I won't worry now about you going as well."

I was intrigued. "Oh?"

"No. We shall both die on the same day, at the same moment, when we are a hundred and two." She paused, and then added, "After Coronation Street. I 'spect Nan will be watching it too."

I was totally disinclined to challenge the logic. Enough that she had rid herself of the grief. And I'm certain the producers of the soap would have been delighted to think they would still be going strong in another forty - or sixty - years depending which of our ages was taken as the benchmark!

Death brings shocks that one hasn't bargained for. Whilst a parent still lives, the fact of one's own mortality doesn't have to be faced. Nan had been the buffer between death and me. With her demise I was next in line, and I feared for my girl. And now I had another challenge. I must live to be a hundred – but with the mind and energy of a fifty year old.

Well, nothing venture, nothing gained.

CHAPTER FIVE

It was shortly after the funeral that a call came from the Social Worker. "There's somewhere I'd like you to go and see. A place has unexpectedly become vacant at Greenlands. Bad timing I know, but you have to seize the opportunity. The chance may not come again. You're very lucky."

It had been planned before Nan had died, for my grandson and his friend to come and stay in the long school holiday, and though so soon after the funeral, I was not disposed to disappoint them. I asked if I could go after their stay, to which she reluctantly agreed.

During the visit of the two teenagers Minty received an invitation to a party from a friend she had known for years. I was surprised, because his father was now dead and his mother in a nursing home. And he too was in a home. The invitation sat on the kitchen shelf for some days before I noticed he was at the same address that the Social Worker had mentioned. Surely fate was taking a hand here and it was a golden opportunity to hear my daughter's first hand impressions. I would drop her off at the party, take Ben and his friend out for the afternoon, and collect her on our way back.

Armed with card and birthday parcel she was greeted by Peter's enveloping arms and a plump smiling carer took them to join the happy buzz of folk who were focussing on the meal preparation taking place in the garden. How lovely that he was to have a party despite not being with family. Definitely a plus sign. When we called later to collect her she had obviously had a thoroughly enjoyable afternoon and greeted me with, "Mum, can I come here. I met nice people and I did like it."

Her request hit me straight between the eyes and the words she had whispered on the day Nan had died were the only ones that made any sense – 'I don't like people all going.'

I told the Social Worker about the birthday party being in the very place there was a vacancy, commented on the incredible coincidence, and that Minty had been very favourably impressed. She said merely, "Good, so she's already seen it."

I should have realised, especially when it had not after all been Peter's birthday - though he had been very happy with the gift! He had just given her an invitation to visit, and there had certainly been a barbeque. From her account of the afternoon there had been a fair number of people there; she had met four members of staff who had introduced themselves and had enjoyed being with them

"Did all the residents invite a guest?" I asked her. Apparently not. Only Peter. Another missed clue. Because it was a summer get together there were more carers on duty than would normally have been the case, and seemingly a lot of residents which didn't tie in with the small number I understood lived there. The staff had obviously made an impression and she would like to go again.

Mind spinning, I was feeling pushed along before adjusting to the most recent assault on our lives.

"We really ought to build on that first success," the Social Worker urged. "Go on to the next stage."

It was only a month since she had told me there was no chance of a residential place as long as I was standing and breathing. Just how many emotional hoops was I to jump through in the space of weeks?

And of course I realised then why she hadn't been surprised when I had told her of the invitation. It had been suggested to Peter, he having been at the same training centre for many years, that he should invite Minty for the special occasion. Staff would then have had a chance to meet and assess her. What could be better than a party atmosphere?

Fair enough, but now I need not be pressured to meet such an imposed pace for I could not stabilise my thinking yet. What agents had been involved for the Manager to know we had been looking at Homes. Who had said what to whom? And did it matter?

The whole prospect of 'doing the right thing' began to drain me of reserves of mental energy. Head battled with heart to respond to the demands of changes to two lives until the bewildering confusion tied me in emotional knots. On tired days I couldn't even change my bed let alone our world. Fear, or was it grief, fluttered constantly around my stomach.

She would go to tea three weeks later; be taken direct from her Centre with those from Greenlands who also attended, and I was to collect her at 6.30pm. Before then I must summon the wherewithal to check every detail that might affect her new life if she continued to want to try living away. She must really have liked the staff for her to become so positive again.

It had been our ultimate objective to protect her from future vulnerability; easy, almost virtuous when it was just an objective, but now faced with such an enormous step, I trembled at the mere thought of it. It would be little short of bereavement, - no, worse, because I not only had to cope with the loss but was responsible for getting the next stage right. Quite the reverse of accepting, as death dictates, that there was nothing more I could do. On the contrary, there was so *much* I must do; one wrong step and a whole life could be disastrously affected. She talked a lot about going; I was the one now to do the acting, whilst supporting her decision.

She seemed quiet when I arrived, and insisted she had enjoyed her stay, but it had obviously lacked the excitement of the Saturday visit with its summer party atmosphere. She liked the carer who had cooked tea, and he and his colleague, who was also 'very kind man', had sat at table with her and joked. It had been suggested by 'another lady' that she return for a special candlelight supper a fortnight later.

"The lady asked what I liked doing and I told her about our candlelight suppers at home on the red check tablecloth," she said, "like we had in Paris, so she said we could do one there and I could help her make it look pretty."

She would too. Sometimes I think we burn more candles than the Vatican!

"I think I'll just practise now," she said, "on our supper table. You can go and write your stories if you like."

It was a familiar hint to disappear. Whenever she had an idea that would give pleasure or delight me, she liked to get on with it undisturbed, and I obliged by going into my study. Some half an hour later she popped her head round the door to ask her if I would show her how to make 'rabbits' ears' with the napkins. It took six or seven attempts to achieve the desired effect, and then deep in concentration she returned to the job in hand.

"All done," she announced. "I can do it now." And then, "Do you think I would be an alcoholic if I had another beer?"
Mystified, for she had rarely drunk beer since Bob had died, I said, "That depends how many you've had."

"I haven't had any yet. I was busy making the table nice."

"In that case you can have another one."
I'm so used to these charmingly illogical conversations that life would lack a dimension if they didn't occur, but I wondered what had sparked off the idea. We always kept a few lagers to hand for visitors; maybe something on the television had reminded her of them.

We were both still anchored to an ongoing and inescapable Peter Pan existence. I was used to replying to a simple question such as 'What time will you come,' by saying, 'When the big hand is on three, get your coat and put everything in your locker. Say goodbye to your friends (long one this!) and when the hand is half way round to four, I'll be there.'

She gives so much more than she takes and caring has never been less than a privilege. Just occasionally I would have given much to have someone else to share the thinking and planning. Someone to provide a respite from the tumult of dealing with the bureaucracy that is inbuilt into a handicapped life; fruitless meetings, referrals and endless phone calls that seemed constantly to surround her. Juggling the demands of the day to participate in assessments of the 'current situation' to indicate 'future need,' and arranging a busy schedule to accommodate visits from officials who then cancel at the last moment or arrive an hour late with plausible excuses but with apparently no understanding of the inconvenience their lateness has caused.

One new initiative follows hard on the heels of another, and with it the requests for information that will be collated on computer to 'provide a better service for all.' The administration, the paperwork, the promises, the quality care and striving for excellence, all somehow disappear in a quagmire of insufficient resources or mismanaged funds and lack of communication.

Yes it would be a welcome change to be able to accept an unscheduled invitation, or concentrate on a talk or film without constantly keeping one eye on my watch. And most of all not having to put on a brave face when I don't *feel* brave, like now, or to pretend things are all right when they are not. In truth to be a couple again, supporting, and covering for each other when the need arises as so frequently it does, to be in two places at the same time.

To shout, to be weak and stop striving without causing Minty pain or distress, for she is intuitively rapid to pick up on any challenge to a serene status quo. I must never give the impression I don't have everything under control because that more than anything, causes anxiety. She needs to know all is well, that the boundaries are intact and everything going to plan.

Later that night I sank dejectedly into the armchair. Truly I was lost, and couldn't see the way ahead. And worse, I couldn't get myself together to decide on a course of action that I was convinced was right, and then stick to it. I see-sawed and vacillated with every wave of emotion, and longed for someone with whom to toss ideas; to weigh pros and cons; to be able to think it through together and give each other strength.

The most difficult adjustment after being part of a couple is to learn to live alone. In marriage one can be alone without feeling lonely whilst widowhood proves the opposite: even when not alone, it feels lonely. Death is radical surgery on the human psyche. All those tiny communications you have as a couple; the 'well done,' 'that's a good idea,' the taking of a hand, or an arm around the shoulder, to signify a support system. These are the street names and familiar landmarks of daily living; the confirmation of being on the right track. Blot them out and you can go round in circles, blindfold and lost in a strange town without a map.

Loneliness thumped relentlessly as I tried to convince myself every angle was being considered, when in reality there was just a spiralling down through a series of negative thoughts. I wanted to be two again; half of a partnership, making plans, sharing decisions, and together accepting the consequences. Two have so much more than double the strength of one, whilst two minus one doesn't equal one, but more often an ineffective insignificant fraction. A million miles separate a mere 'I', and a safe, secure 'us'. Two together can take on the world. And oh how one misses the laughter; the audible mirth of a shared joke. Smiling silently and alone at an amusing situation on the television is no substitute.

I reflected on the number of times I have been urged by well meaning friends, to marry again. 'You have a life too,' they say, assuming being 'one' means that Mr. Right must automatically ring my doorbell every morning. 'So and so is on *his* own' as if that's all the qualification needed to form a partnership. 'He enjoys books and theatre too....' I reign in my irritation or amusement, depending on the day, and to myself think, 'Damn the hobbies, we have to get into bed together. Nineteen or ninety we need the chemistry too! Surely compatibility is the most essential element if marriage is to survive. All the rest is a matter of compromise; of giving and taking.'

As for 'having a life too', I *do* have a life. It may be unlike anything I imagined as a young woman; in fact totally different in every respect from the one envisaged, but a good life nonetheless. It's not what some might consider a balanced one, but that's all right. And often I feel I have a richer life than most; for in being a carer, one is unconsciously trained to observe minutiae of moments that might otherwise go unheeded and undervalued. In opening the eyes of another, one learns how to see. And loving with the intense love that responds to another's need, my world so often shrinks to what seems the intended size containing small islands of peace, each with the quality of a gem.

The trust between carer and cared for is steel-strong; an exclusive, unconditional two way loving, often incomprehensible to an outsider who sees only the apparent catastrophe. Life is no longer a travelling from A to B whilst acquiring the maximum en route, but a journey of discovery; a series of unexpected, small miracles. It's a progress, not a station; our destination a matter of uncertainty.

Yes of course it would be a relief not to have to worry about car repairs or house insurance, getting the lawnmower to start and fixing a blocked washing machine. To have someone to phone after a journey and say, 'I've arrived safely,' confident the news will be welcome because love is involved. Not having to carry a big handbag everywhere because there are male pockets to hold money, keys, cheque books and tickets etc. In short, to be cared for in the marital sense. Such a tempting comfort to lean now and then on someone who could take the strain of daily living for a while, instead of being the one to reassure, provide answers, to make life all right again.

But not at any price. And most definitely not at a price to my girl.

And like other widows I sometimes feel the urge to strangle those smug females who without an atom of sensitivity delight in shrilling, "Oh my husband does all that - I wouldn't have a clue." And then immediately taking credit for the success of what she doesn't have a clue about, 'Of course we've got our home in the sun, a good pension (his)..... We drove to the south of France this year. You should try it; it's really quite easy. Well yes there were two to drive but he preferred to do it, and it's a company car, so no danger of expensive breakdowns......'

There are many who enjoy proving they have no need of 'a mere male'; they can do it better anyway. I'm not one of them and would give much to be important to someone. But I know too that though it would be reassuring to have someone with whom to grow old, someone to share the discovery that daily living is not the simple automatic exercise it once was, my head knows that for me it's not a case of remaining one or becoming two; I'm either single or we become three, and it's no secret that three's a crowd.

However well intentioned, whatever the resolve or depth of love, one day resentment would surface and I would be tugged in two directions, and, worse, those on either side would be hurt. It's inconceivable to contemplate marrying someone and telling him he could never come first in my life. He'd have to be superhuman for it not to matter. It's not the way I would have chosen things to be; it's the way things *are* because of the dependence involved.

And it's certainly not the fault of my Peter Pan for what did she ever do to be born with such a handicap to living. She's not a petulant child refusing to allow her father's place to be usurped, or jealous of what another might take that should one day be hers. She doesn't waste time on assessing or manipulating human contrariness and shows her emotions openly and with sincerity.

The last thing in the world she would want is to restrict my life for she loves in a most remarkable way that no 'normal' person could ever love. So genuine, hers is an unshakeable love that never falters or weakens, and is everything described in the passage from Corinthians, read at so many marriage services.

Often I marvel at the power of it. She generates such intensity of affection that there is a corresponding desire to plumb the unfathomable needs of a handicapped child. She clearly wants me to be happy; does a multitude of things to brighten my life, is totally unselfish, and incapable of being self centred or envious. When I'm happy then so is she. But it would destroy her to feel an obstacle or in the way. She's not capable of imagining that marriage to someone other than her father could ever be a problem for she would assume the same uncomplicated and unconditional love as her own.

And I'm too much the coward to take the risk.

* * *

So here we were at the most significant crossroad of our lives and must decide the direction that would affect us for always. Longing for approval and confirmation, I struggled to find the way forward; the way that would be best for everyone in the family if I were to fall off my perch precipitately. And though I didn't recognise it at the time, I still needed to grieve a mother I'd had for long enough to become a 'wrinklie' myself.

Before any decision, there were many visits to be made, questions to be asked and issues to be resolved – before and after the candlelight supper. Many times I made appointments to call, and each time the Manager made me welcome, listened to my concerns and responded with the assurances I seemed to need as we sat in the residents' chintzy airy sitting room, - one I would have been content to have for my own. I told him of the coincidence of Minty being invited to the birthday party that wasn't, and he smiled but didn't contradict my impression. We talked about the staff and he was proud that his were a cut above the average. He was able to pay a little more and had therefore a greater number of applicants from whom to choose.

All was spotlessly clean. The room Minty would have was a good size and with a pleasant outlook through French windows overlooking the garden. Currently it was without a carpet, but soon there would be one to match the new décor, for amazingly she could meet with the decorator, look at wallpaper samples, and choose her own colour scheme prior to moving in. She would love that, and would probably choose pink and grey as in her room at home for she is not a great one for change once she has found something to her liking.

Relatives of the previous occupant had left a portable TV, which meant she could watch her favourite soaps, either here, or in one of the two sitting rooms. Apparently she could use either, and I guessed she would prefer the one in which I usually met Mr. Brown. She could bring pieces of furniture from home if she wished, if that helped her to settle in more quickly. There didn't seem to be anything they hadn't thought of and I was beginning to feel more comfortable with the situation. The sensible part of me knew we were fortunate to have found them, (or for them to have found us,) even if the emotional part was having difficulty letting go. But if this was where she was going to be happy, I would handle the emotional problems in the privacy of home. Of that there was no question.

I was eager to discuss medication and diet, for the administration of these would be crucial to her settling in. Please, I was pleading silently as I got the measure of him, don't feed me bureaucratic responses. Feel for me. Feel *with* me, as I come to terms with letting you share the greatest possible gift.

Please understand how this is tearing me apart; how, because I have cared for her and lived her life with her for so long, I literally can't separate us. The edges are so blurred, so lacking in definition I have trouble knowing which pieces fit into whose puzzle. I need help to discover how to leave me in one place whilst she comes to another, not just physically, but emotionally and spiritually.

Such private thoughts of course remained unexpressed.

* * *

There was a fair amount of medication involved. Minty could administer her own, for our doctor and I had spent years teaching her how to recognise her need, and with those tablets she needed daily, a routine had been developed. It was absolutely essential that all were kept in their packets for she could recognise the large printed name of the pills on each - the only word she could see as her vision is very poor. I had highlighted the names in different colours with which she was familiar. One prescription had recently been reduced to alternate days. This was quite difficult even for normal person to remember so it was easier to break tablets in halves for her to take each morning.

Another was more complicated in that she must take as and when she felt the need in response to spasms, the time of which could not be predicted, but in general the safe guide was up to three over a twenty-four hour period. She had learnt to recognise the signs a tablet was needed, and must always have them with her for whatever hour of day or night they were required. I asked that she be allowed to continue the independence she had developed at home, something that was readily agreed to during our discussions over several weeks.

I was to write everything down clearly and Mr. Brown suggested a medicine cupboard or box that Minty could keep in her room. He was confident that such a degree of independence would be well received and admired by those administratively responsible for Greenlands. I was relieved by such an attitude, for if Minty's medicine were to be administered by staff as though she were a patient in hospital, her independence, and thus confidence in herself, would take a nosedive. Indeed it would be a serious retrograde step, and the loss of years of training.

The box would be ordered and ready for her arrival, he said.

* * *

Very early on in our meetings, I had sought, and was given, a promise that she could continue her 'job' as classroom assistant at a children's nursery some six miles from Greenlands. This would entail a member of staff driving her there each Friday morning after breakfast, and if it couldn't be done I must know now before making any commitment. The continuation of the project was essential given the immense difference it had made to her self esteem; indeed it would have been counter productive for it to end. And on the occasions she planned to come home for the weekend I would collect her at the end of the nursery school session, thus saving staff one of the journeys. Given the drive would take a staff member from base, I wondered if might this be a problem. Not at all.

Minty had no special dietary needs such as would be dictated by say diabetes etc, but for her well being we had spent the past two years enjoying a healthy balanced diet that excluded high fat foods. She was delighted by a significant weight loss over this lengthy period, looked trimmer, felt better, took a pride in her appearance and was much less lethargic than when heavy. There was no need of a special diet, just adherence to a healthy one and I sought assurance that this could be maintained. And Mr. Brown's face lit up as if having an idea vindicated.

It was, he said, to make sure that each client ate according to individual need that he had decided against having a cook who would expect all residents to eat the same menu (unless a medical condition precluded this), and at same time. A number of staff members loved cooking and thus Minty would be catered for as an individual with her own diet. She could even go shopping with them to purchase grocery items. That was what finally swayed me for it seemed that she would get the attention to her nutrition that I gave her at home. She would enjoy shopping and given help with the oven dial that she couldn't see, would make a simple healthy stir-fry, or casserole.

I asked him to understand that it would all be a learning curve for me, undoubtedly a painful one, and I hoped he would tell me if and when I went about things the wrong way. I wouldn't be offended, but grateful for his guidance, for we both had my daughter's interests at heart.

I drove back less anxious, a stirring of feeling that her future could be as safe in other hands as my own: something that simultaneously relieved, and hurt. She might be happy, grow even, without me, and my constant attention.

At home I congratulated her on finding the right place. She had done it all alone on the day she went to Peter's party. I had spent years looking for what she had found so easily. Such coincidences should be heeded for they did not occur often.

We talked long and often, and having decided to give it a try, knew it was time to tell family. Getting to this point had been an emotional marathon in itself and I didn't bargain for the reactions that followed. I suppose it was naïve to assume that everyone would realise how tortuous and draining had been the decision, even more that they would be supportive whilst we ventured on such life changing territory. Nan had always been our fiercest opposition, but having accompanied us on some visits, had realised that the places she envisaged belonged to her own childhood. And then, just before dying, had agreed after all it might be for the best, and must at least be tried.

I was dumbfounded by the range of opinion expressed. Some thought I should have made such a move years earlier instead of hanging onto my girl like 'some over-possessive mother' whilst others, mildly or vehemently, expressed disbelief that I could even think of 'abandoning her.'

I was ill prepared for such reaction and numbed by the lack of understanding of what the decision had cost; had mistakenly assumed their support despite differing viewpoints. Guilt now lay as heavy as lead and I could barely drag myself through the days that followed. Whatever I did I was selfish and uncaring in someone's eyes, reactions that completely knocked the stuffing out of me.

A friend whose handicapped son had died recently was far less inhibited, and reacted bitterly. "And those who care so much have phoned her regularly, have they? Or invited her to stay the weekend or taken her on a holiday? They are so numerous these people who do nothing but judge, but my God how their hearts bleed!"

Her anger boiled over, and I knew she was reliving what must have been a tortuous situation for her.

CHAPTER SIX

I had slept only fitfully, and woke with a boulder where my heart should have been. Today Minty would go for a stopover; the beginning of the change to the rest of out lives. We were to arrive about eleven on Saturday morning and I was to collect her after lunch on Sunday. We were getting ever nearer to the end of our life together, a life that had been lived in many ways more closely than a married couple, due the dependence and vulnerability of the one, and the profound love she evoked in the other.

Human beings are really very fragile emotionally and the strength I had developed over four decades to keep two serenely afloat now began to desert me. I must be positive, keep smiling, because for Minty it would be a move forward - like going off to university, or getting married. Except that it couldn't be like that for her, because the Never Never Land she belongs to has precluded becoming properly adult. And now we had started to grow comparatively old together and I couldn't imagine living life in any other way.

Had I left it too late to avoid pain for her? It would have been more natural for her to go when her brothers left home – but they married close to the time her father suffered cancer. In those devastating months of watching a disease steal the life from him, she had woken every two hours in the night with me to turn his fragile body. Together, because it was unavoidable, we watched his cruel decline and final demise.

Finding a Home and dealing with the bureaucracy surrounding such a move, had been the last thing on my mind. But two years later we had discovered Home Farm, the only place I deemed good enough for such a precious person, and the one irrevocably ruled out by our county council. Then had followed 'Community Care' and a raft of new ideas and political initiatives, none of which had done other than to shake the ground beneath us.

* * *

The young carer appointed to be Minty's 'special person' received us. She was obviously newly appointed and we warmed to each other in a way that suggested we were sharing, albeit at opposite ends of the spectrum, a daunting and unfamiliar experience. Words locked in my throat and I was incapable of saying anything sensible or coherent.

I sensed they would get on well together and felt a superficial relief skim the surface of my desolation. She would, she said, be with Minty until 2pm, when she was due to go off duty, but would make sure she was happily settled with her replacement. Meanwhile they would make lunch together. I wished I'd known she would go off duty so soon after Minty's arrival for then I could have taken her earlier for them to become better acquainted, and wondered why no-one had mentioned this. However I was impressed to learn that Mr. Brown had arranged to be on night duty as it was Minty's first time to sleep here. I would thank him when I called next morning.

She was quiet when I arrived a minute before the appointed time but said she loved the staff and had had a nice time with them. The bed had been comfy but too slippery and I assumed it had been a hospital type mattress of which she had no need.

Many months later she showed me her diary to help produce this book. We've always written them together each evening before going to bed, a habit she obviously continued in the weeks she was away. This was her entry with spelling corrected, as with subsequent ones, to assist the reader:-

'After Jane left it felt strange. I sat in bedroom and Joe helped me get a programme. He ate supper with Hugh and me. Hugh is staff, and nice. After supper I went back to my room because Peter was watching Millionaire and I don't understand that programme. I wish

47

it was time for Mum to come. I went to bed early. Mr. Brown did not come and see me. He shone a torch in my room later on. He thought I was sleep. I kept waking. I heard someone slam a door and someone talking and saying 'Ssh Minty is sleeping, but I wasn't. It feels strange without mum. I love her so much. We had cooked breakfast. I sat with Peter Robert and Emily to have breakfast and went back to the room. Sarah made lunch. I like her. She sat with me to eat. I happy again. My mum will soon be here. Jane is gone now.'

On the way home she told me how much she liked Mr. Brown but she wished he had talked with her. I explained, as nearly as would make sense to her that he really couldn't go into her room and chat in the middle of the night without getting into trouble.

"But he was the Manager. How could he be in trouble with himself, and wasn't he there to look after her?" she asked, simplifying with a stroke all that today's society has complicated. With litigation forever lurking in the background, the sad activities of the nefarious few have put the conscientious ones ever more carefully on their guard. It is the necessary way of the modern world.

She rang her young carer to thank her and mentioned the bed. It would be replaced with a new one, she was promised, as soon as residency had been agreed.

The next invitation came for a supper early in December, with an indication that an offer for residency to begin on the 14th would be made. She looked forward to Mr. Brown asking her to go to his office for him to make the formal offer rather as if she had passed an entrance exam.

"We shall be doing business," she told me buoyantly. "And then I shall come home and have a *finanxious* meeting Mum, to arrange the money I need to go out for coffees and things."

I have always loved her version of 'financial'; it so much more aptly describes the feelings people generally experience when discussing money!

Instinct suggested it might be helpful for him to know what importance she was placing on such a formality, and he might welcome such 'information' to keep her on board, for it would be so

48

easy for her to lose her nerve at this stage. And so I was thrown when he called back some half hour later saying that his Deputy, not he personally, would be making the offer of a place in the way I had understood. The bureaucratic reason he gave, which ten minutes later I interpreted as 'stepping on someone's toes' disturbed me, but I couldn't at that moment isolate this unease from the overwhelming reluctance to let her go. He was in charge. I was mystified.

During this conversation it became clear that he had overall management for not one, but two homes, and in his absence from either, there were two Deputies in charge. The offer must come from the one at Greenlands. In all the visits I had made I had never met the lady, which seemed odd, but I was too desperately trying to curb the powerful urge to say we had changed our minds to challenge him. And of course *we* hadn't. I was the one losing my nerve.

Even with that information I never dreamt that he wouldn't have the last word on everything, for it was he who had met with me on each visit, he who had listened and given the necessary assurances. I had not in fact exchanged a word with the Deputy who may indeed be the most wonderful person, but I should have been introduced if she was to be in charge of my daughter. And surely she would have wished to meet with me? Or was I irrelevant?

Suddenly all our discussions became meaningless and I rang to voice my concern. I was placated somewhat on hearing that they liased on all matters and ran Greenlands according to the agreed policy, a copy of which I had been given.

I had asked a family friend of long standing to accompany me when collecting Minty after the supper, and to look around and ask any questions that came to mind that I hadn't already raised. She showed him the room she would have, and though having previously been so thrilled with it, I picked up the merest shred of unease in her, though she insisted all was well. I communicated my observation to our friend, who was most favourably impressed. He would, he said, were he in the same position, feel very fortunate to have found it and would have no hesitation in a member of his family living there.

"Think you might be looking for problems?" he teased. "Look at her now!"

Indeed she was chatting animatedly to Mr. Brown, who gave her his undivided attention, and was evidently suggesting that she move in on the December 17th, a few days later than initially suggested, but with enough time to settle in before Christmas. They were laughing as I heard her say delightedly, "Yes that's fine. I'll come. We are doing good business together aren't we!"

Long after she came home again, I read her diary entry. The evening was so indelibly etched on her mind that her impressions were clearly detailed.

"After the supper I wanted to go to Mr. Brown's office for him to tell me I come and live here. But he didn't and I heard Mrs. Quin telling Stephanie I be moving in. I wanted have important interview about it but they didn't talk to me at all about it. After Mum came I talked to Mr Brown. Then it was important.

I only sensed on the night, because I hadn't then seen her diary, that they had lost a little of her confidence, and though she couldn't express it, she felt they undervalued her in so far as she was not part of the agreement with its offer and acceptance procedure. Perhaps I was being unreasonable. It would take a long time for them to get to know her as I did; to read every nuance and reaction. Later, as I grew to know the other residents, I sensed it was perhaps because she was more capable than some. For them such involvement would have been irrelevant, especially if they had come to Greenlands as a result of a parent's death.

We bought things for her new room and she looked forward to choosing the decoration of it, and once installed, asking me to tea 'at her place.' She might even invite me for Christmas if there were going to be lots of parties, she said, or she might come home. It would depend... she would see how things turned out. That someone who had embodied the spirit of Christmas for over forty years, someone who had kept us believing in Father Christmas and his appetite for mince pies, not because she actually did believe, but because she *preferred* to believe, might not be at my table, did not bear thinking about.

50

But if inviting me to have lunch with her made her feel independent and on an equal footing with the rest of the world then I must adjust to the new demands for that was what leaving home was all about. With her I enthused about the possibility whilst surprising myself with a talent for acting. The misery that seemed to get inside every nerve and sinew was for times I was alone.

Whilst I was spiralling down she was flying, and I must fly with her if I was to do what must be done in helping her to 'cross a bridge' from home to as near independent living as was possible for her, before I was no longer around. And why was I so gutted by the prospect if this was what we had been seeking for seventeen years? Except it wasn't because it was a Home rather than a village with home, workplace and leisure pursuits securely adjacent, as Home Farm had been. But Minty had found it, liked it, and asked to go there. She could go to her Centre each day as before, and it was also near enough for me to drop by as often as she wanted. We had been very lucky.

So why didn't it feel that way?

* * *

There were more residents and staff than we had expected when she next went to supper - a special occasion when both homes managed by Mr. Brown were to share a Christmas meal. In such a convivial atmosphere, Minty quickly released my hand as she saw staff she had met on previous visits. I recognised the secure feeling of 'I'm fine Mum – you can go now.'

I took my cue and left the party girl on the inside whilst only a few steps into the outside, I felt my world collapsing. An enormous void was opening in front of me. After forty years I couldn't imagine days without her and wished I could put a name to the feelings that raged; it would have made them more tolerable. Tonight she had demonstrated her readiness to leave me and in three hours I must return with a face glowing to match hers.

I drove home to a house echoing with emptiness, and with the absence of someone who could understand. Unable to settle to anything, I paced the floor for wasteful minutes, then took a hot bath to pass the time before collecting her. Numerous times I had laughed when she said, 'I leave all my worries in the bath – I can see them running away with the bubbles!'

Mine didn't. They floated menacingly on the surface, mocking my attempts to dispel them. It felt like bereavement all over again and memories flooded back of Bob's consultant telling me that 'it couldn't be long now', and then staying awake, trying to hold back the hours from their race towards the inevitable end.

Having returned early, I sat outside in the car park almost full with the cars of visitors and staff from both homes. Deep down this had been last hope she might change her mind for I was now no longer planning intelligently, but taken over by emotions I could neither understand nor control. I locked the car and plastered a resolute smile on my face before going in, and hoped the fragility of my composure would not be tested.

In the general melée of seasonal excitement, I was introduced to the staff in general who said, "Happy Christmas – you won't remember names etc." I caught a sensitive smile from one whom I thought said she was the Deputy. I sensed she was giving me a boost and I nodded gratefully. My girl would be all right with her.

The visiting group were getting into coats now, and bundling parcels into bags, and Mr. Brown beckoned me into the corridor. The decorator would be here next week, and Minty could call in to choose her decoration. All would be ready for the 17th. It would give her a week to settle in before Christmas. He seemed to assume she would want to come home for the festival itself.

* * *

She had looked forward to meeting the decorator, and choosing pink and white daisies from his sample book. But when we arrived on the day arranged, there were just a few sample bits left in an envelope on her bed, hurriedly torn from no doubt larger pieces that had been collected from the DIY store because Minty must have mentioned pink on one of her visits. Her 'special carer' had responded to our ringing of the doorbell and explained that all members of staff were in a meeting, though we had arrived at the time agreed. Jane was young and fresh and Minty warmed to her arm around her shoulder.

She not only didn't like the designs that reflected an older choice, but was picking up the fact that she wasn't here to discuss patterns in the way she had expected, and to have fun doing so. She said nothing and I could feel her shrinking from both them, and the situation. Jane picked up on her mood and said, "I'm not keen on them either. Look, the decorator is painting the bathroom - let's go and have a word with him." But someone came out of the staff meeting to recall her and hastily indicating where we should go, she apologised, and left us.

I tried to rationalise and help us both to accept that the world didn't revolve around one person - maybe the first lesson on what leaving home was about. Reactions were in overdrive again. Was I looking for reasons for her not to come?

The decorator had his brush in a pot of peach paint and was making a superb job of the bathroom, but looked at us blankly when we asked for a sample book. "'Fraid I can't help you love."

"I like that colour," Minty said. "Better than the wallpaper.'
I felt they had let her down somewhat despite someone having rushed to B&Q prior to our arrival. Stupid of me not to have realised that all the rooms would be decorated on a rolling programme and each resident would probably go out with his or her carer to choose paint and paper. Minty, as the new resident had happened to come at a time coinciding with main rooms being decorated and thus hers could be done while the decorator was on site. As she didn't yet live in, there had apparently been a last minute dash to give her the promised choice.

Everyone was installed in the meeting so I suggested to the decorator that if she really preferred paper, for I feared she had settled for peach rather than put anyone to any trouble, I would take her into town on Saturday to choose some.

"You'd have to have it back by tomorrow, I'm afraid. I won't be in at the weekend," he said apologetically. "Why didn't they ask you to get it last week - they knew I was coming on Monday."

Another indication, and in giving them the benefit of the doubt I missed it. I was drained. Mr. Brown was not there, and none in authority was hovering to help.

"The peach would be nice Mum," Minty said. "I like it."

"And easier for me," the decorator said with his eye on his watch. "I could make a start tomorrow."

"Yes please," she said, deciding matters. And if she were still positive, I must keep in mind her obvious fondness for her new carer.

With hindsight I saw it as a significant lost opportunity to bond with the new incumbent; a promise kept according to a policy document, but not with commitment and understanding. Choosing the decoration of one's new home was significant. Why invite us when there was noone available to talk, unless it was a case of the right hand not knowing what the left had did; something that didn't fit with the Deputy.

It was only later that I learned that the lady who had smiled encouragingly on the night of the festive celebration, was indeed the Deputy - but from the *other* home. Minty's Deputy was the lady who had recalled Jane into the staff meeting, and of whom I had only caught a glimpse.

In his absence, I left a note thanking Mr. Brown for the promise he had given over the past weeks that she could continue her job at the Day Nursery, and that staff would be able to take her. I would collect her whenever she came home for the weekend. Given today's discovery of mistaken identity, instinct urged that I sought confirmation of this agreement.

Next day I received a call. "I'm sorry but we're going to have to delay entry for a couple of days, to the 19th - a few minor difficulties. But everything will be ready by Wednesday." The female voice was pleasant enough, but so casual, and seemed unaware what reserves of mental energy had been consumed getting ready to say goodbye on a certain date, only to have it delayed for a second time as if it were a clinic appointment.

The new date was so close to the Christmas weekend, giving only two days in which to settle in rather than a whole week as planned. All the pressure from Social Services for me to make a decision because 'the place couldn't be held forever,' and they were the ones not ready.

CHAPTER SEVEN

With the entry delayed I fought to quell tears that manifested at surprising moments. What on earth was I doing? I was about to lose the most precious person and in doing so was forfeiting that private space around my deepest self where I was in control against any invading hurt; could already feel the destruction. *But it wasn't about me.* Minty wanted to try living independently - something I thought might not happen again so long after being refused when she was twenty-seven.

Together we were doing it to protect her future, and to avoid the trauma of losing a parent and her home and all that was familiar at one and the same moment; to help her over a bridge so that she wouldn't have to do it alone and my sons would not have to care for an ageing, handicapped sister whose eventual deterioration would make the kind of demands that could wreck a marriage.

I tried to imagine the husband to whom I'd made that promise, alongside again, and knew without a doubt he would have said, 'We've come this far – don't buckle now.' I must focus on the objective and hold firm. Without him I was lopsided and lame.

Out of the blue on the 18th, we received a call to say one of Minty's brothers was in London on business - he would make a flying visit next day before returning to the continent.

"She's really perky about it," he commented. "Bubbling."

And I knew then why I had allowed the wallpaper business and the delayed date to go unchallenged.

Smiling encouragingly next day, I literally bit my lip all the way there. Minty was a little quiet and apprehensive, which was only to be expected. But her eyes lit up when Mr. Brown greeted us and

56

she saw her room, now delightful in peach and cream. Vases of flowers offering a delicious scent, and cards of welcome, covered the surfaces. It was going to be all right.

"I can unpack Mum," she said. She was already opening her bag of photographs and putting them on shelves.

"Hint taken." I forced a laugh, marvelling that the words actually came out of my mouth.

I went to the office and told Mr. Brown we had brought all her medication in the box she normally kept in her bedside table at home - a decorative one she was specially fond of because of the three apricot coloured flowers on the top. No doubt he would want to transfer everything to the medicine box or cabinet he had ordered. However that hadn't arrived yet, and he was openly pleased we had brought one with us. I explained that it didn't lock, but the fact that we had brought one seemed to suffice.

I had noticed immediately the absence of the promised carpet, though there was nothing wrong with the meticulously polished floor. The Deputy with whom I had as yet only spoken over the phone when she called to delay entry, joined us and was introduced as Mrs. Quin. Irrationally I was still shocked at her not being the person who had smiled on the party night.

"We thought Minty might like to choose her own carpet," she said. "As you know the decorating has only just been completed." As if she had sensed the reaction to the wallpaper samples, she said that commercial sample books of carpet would be coming from the housing association and she expected one would be fitted by the time Minty returned after coming home for Christmas.

"Enjoy unpacking and call me if you need anything - I'm in the office," she called over her shoulder.

And in the tense state I was in, I didn't know if those cheerfully spoken words were ones of compassion, or professional integrity.

"I'll go home and get some rugs until your carpet comes," I said. "I'll be back to see your new room." I tried to say 'home' but room was all I could manage.

The Deputy, who had overheard, reappeared. "I was thinking - I've got a rug I could bring in if you don't feel like driving home."

If she had, I wondered why she hadn't brought it in already. And would she remember tomorrow if she hadn't thought of it today? I was beginning to get an impression of an assured and unworried personality. Perfectly pleasant, open, and helpful but at the moment of need, rather than due the forethought I would have imagined imperative in her position. But I was hardly in a rational state of mind myself - how at this moment could my judgement of anyone's character be reliable. I was about to leave when Minty appeared in the corridor.

"Mum do you think I'd be allowed to take this plastic off my mattress?"

I went to her room and saw, now that she pulled back the duvet, that the 'hospital' mattress was still in situ, albeit practically a new one, and functional for the previous occupant. But it *had* been agreed to replace it.

"And of course we will," Mrs. Quin smiled. "It's all been such a rush to have everything finished."

I didn't understand. We would have been totally cooperative - I more than delighted - about waiting until after Christmas if that had been more convenient, but the Social Worker had continually given the impression that it was something of a luxury to take so long before making a final decision, and by November was putting the pressure on. "All the time the room stands empty, funds are being drained from the budget," she had persisted.

Weighed against my instinct to return Minty and all her belongings to the car saying that we would come back when everything was ready, was the unnerving effect it might have on her, for she was still happily arranging her pictures and certificates.

Mr. Brown gestured to me to join him. "Why doesn't she have a complete new bed," he suggested. "One of your own choice."
He was either rescuing a situation, or embarrassed by the oversight. The amount he offered was generous and would ensure top quality, and it was agreed I would go into town next day, and purchase and arrange to have one delivered. Meanwhile I would drive home and get a rug for the floor and an extra duvet to soften the 'hospital' mattress.

58

Before leaving I gave him a typed list of her medication, indicating what each tablet was for, the dosage and the times Minty would take them. She had everything with her and knew exactly what to do and the pills could be transferred to the lockable box when it was to hand.

It didn't occur to me that it might not yet have been ordered.

"Best use the one she's used to for the time being," Mr Brown said, and I reminded him that she could read the names of the pills which was in large print on the packaging, but quite unable to read the much smaller print on the foil backing of each strip of tablets.

He looked at my list and the specific information I had provided.

"Excellent - no room for any misunderstanding there. It's all very clear. I'll have a copy made for each member of staff. And thank you." He smiled warmly and I felt steadier if somewhat frayed at the edges.

On separate sheets I had added any background information that might be helpful – how she liked to have her bedroom door open at night and to have a dim light in the corridor. The latter would be no problem because it was statutory for the night staff. I had, on several occasions tried to ease her door closed a few inches to shield her from the light, but even though she was fast asleep, she awoke, sensitive to the change, waited for me to disappear so that I wouldn't be 'hurt' and then reopened it.

I had explained too, that 'anxiety' was her middle name and avoidance of it would have a tremendous effect on her well-being. But that required advance thinking; something that was now as natural to me as breathing. And too, how she loved tidiness and an ordered lifestyle. A structured routine was vital.

For many years now her day has begun predictably. On waking she takes her medication, pauses at the window on the stairs to check the weather, and then en route for breakfast, turns over the page in the Radio Times ready for her evening viewing. She eats her cereal and checks the bag she has packed the previous evening ready for the day's activities.

Before leaving for her Centre, she gives me a prolonged hug and asks what we'll be having for dinner. Probably, in the new circumstances she would also ask who would be on duty when she returned. With all now in order, she can fill in the first part of the day's diary entry! Any change to the routine daily viewing, such as a major international football match, is an irritation and not worthy of comment!

She would love me to watch all her soaps with her but we compromise, settling for her favourite Coronation Street and Neighbours. The programmes provide a base for discussion and I encourage her to project possibilities, reason what the outcomes will be, and to suggest solutions to the endless domestic dramas that arise. They have been invaluable in extending her limited vocabulary, developing her questioning skill and ability to offer alternatives.

Her viewing has also kept me aware of the level of her understanding over the years, and provided a measure of her concentration. Both reached a peak in her late twenties but the latter has diminished significantly in the mid forties.

Sometimes, she opens the door between the TV room and kitchen, so that 'you can enjoy the other soaps Mum whilst you prepare dinner. Then you won't miss anything exciting.'
I confess to closing the door another inch at every opportunity, preferring to listen to the radio. But I'm sure that friends who are too polite to comment, are surprised by my 'in depth' knowledge of the goings on in Weatherfield and Ramsay Street!

Often now, she retains only the superficial storyline, innuendo and sarcasm totally escaping her. She has always taken everything that is said at face value, but instinct has often helped her to recognise the 'bad characters.' Over the years, tolerance and understanding of weakness, even murder, has increased, for these people are her friends and extended family, and 'the pressures on them must be understood.' Regular as clockwork she meets with them; sees them hurting or happy, and from the kitchen I hear her giving them advice, and the benefit of her longer experience!

"Calm down. Just wait patiently," she will say, "and it will all be fine. Just give him time and he *will* ask you to marry him."

There might be a little bit of self-comforting in some of her remarks, for she has yearned for Mr Right to materialise and sweep her off her feet. Observation however confirms that she is older than her years, ageing prematurely now, and it is as if she has at last settled for what is, and has let go of the 'what may be round the corner'. Safe, secure, and familiar is now the order of the day. She has recognised for a long time that she is 'different,' and that her handicap prohibits what others enjoy, which is of course the downside to being a less severe Downs.

I was listening intently one evening to a particularly articulate speaker on 'Any Questions' when the door was flung open, and a concerned daughter called out, "You should have seen how cross his Mum was. She was shouting and throwing things!"

"But what had he done?" I asked, pretending I knew the object of her concern.

"She's furious because he's got green body and arms!"
I was mystified. "You mean he poured paint all over himself?"

"No, no. He's gone to the police station and then he'll go to prison and his Mum won't be able to tuck him in any more nights and I 'spect she'll be sad."

I sought a few more clues. The 'He' wasn't an infant let loose with a paint pot, but a young thug who had injured an old lady whilst robbing her pension, and presumably to be subsequently charged with *grievous bodily harm!*

Intriguing this complete lack of intellectual curiosity. She could accept what she thought was 'green body' without need for the evidence of colour, yet at times seems to have the instinctive wisdom of Solomon. She doesn't think in logical patterns, and yet her world, on the one hand so limited, is in other ways wide and complex, and never ceases to surprise me.

* * *

I sought another 'favour' on her behalf for she only enjoys hot food if served on a hot plate. It is terribly important to her and detracts wholly from her enjoyment if either is allowed to go cold. I approached in it jocular manner but left them in no doubt that as far as she was concerned, their reputation would be made, or would flounder, on this maxim. All the others requests were for her fundamental safety and well-being: this one would affect her daily quality of life, and determine her approval or otherwise of the place, and thus her ability to adjust.

The Manager smiled. "If that's all we have to do to please her, you have nothing to worry about," he laughed. "I'm sure we can cope with such a modest request."

"Modest, but essential to her," I said earnestly.

I explained the small expenses that would be required on a weekly basis when she attended the Centre. Money for yoga, riding and a small amount for a subsidised college lunch - about ten pounds in all. Thursday was her day off and on Fridays no money was needed when she went to work at the Day Nursery from where I would collect her for the weekend, when again she would have no need of cash.

It had been agreed that coming home for weekends was the best way to ease her in gently.

She needed more sleep these days, rather in the manner of a person ageing and found it impossible to sustain a five-day week, hence the day off when she would probably take an afternoon nap. Not capable of doing her own laundry, being unable to see the dials on the washing machine, she nevertheless enjoyed unloading the machine and helping to hang clothes out to dry. She could do simple ironing if the thermostat were to be set at the correct temperature, and her room would always be impeccably clean.

Such background information would I hoped, help them to get to know her sooner, eliminate avoidable stresses, and aid the settling in process.

The phone was ringing as I put my key in the door. It was Stephanie, the administrator of the Housing Association who had visited us twice over the previous weeks and I had appreciated her compassionate efficiency. She had explained that Minty would in law be renting at Greenlands, but that until her allowance book was signed over to them, I was to continue cashing her allowances and then send the appropriate cheque to the Housing Association. Allowances would currently only cover rent and food for evidently I had not been claiming all to which she was entitled. Had she been in receipt of the full amount, there would have been an additional small sum for her personal expenses. Stephanie would see that this was rectified, but warned it would take time.

As a tenant she could end her tenancy whenever she wished by giving the appropriate notice or rent in lieu. So by giving it a try we would lose nothing: if it proved not to be right for her, there was no lengthy commitment to be honoured. Though this came as an enormous relief, we had nonetheless embarked on the scheme very seriously and with total commitment to making it work.

"You've done it!" she said. "Has she enjoyed moving in?"

I told her we were still in the process, and about the carpet and the bed, but that the latter was now in hand. Although professionally disguised, her annoyance was evident. "Goodness me I assumed the bed had already been replaced. And Minty's room could have been decorated first so that she could have moved in on the 14th as arranged. The delay can't have been easy for either of you. And are you sure you are all right getting the bed? Yes I will take carpet samples in, but not tomorrow, and no it won't be laid so quickly. Nobody will be working over Christmas."

Should I be recognising an attitude at the top that was too 'laid back,' or were they just teething problems? I mustn't overlook the many cards of welcome that had awaited Minty's arrival, or the vases of flowers and little gifts on her bedside table from staff with whom she had yet to become properly acquainted. Their action said much about them. Confused and fraught on an emotional see-saw, I didn't feel I could trust my own judgement.

I had asked whether I should make an advance payment on her rent, but the Housing Officer had said that until a rent book was received from the finance department for rent to be paid on a weekly basis, I was not to worry, and wait for an invoice. To that end I put her entire allowance into the bank so that payment could be dealt with as soon as requested. Meanwhile the Manager had suggested I make an interim deposit of a hundred pounds with Greenlands from which Minty could draw personal money each week as and when needed.

I filled the boot of the car and returned to find her room already looked lived in and to my delight, a daughter who had enjoyed making it so. Someone called Grace had come on duty whilst I had been home, and had helped her with her duvet and bed making 'to give Mum a nice surprise when she came back'.

But she was tired now and excitement was waning; the first signs appearing of apprehension about my going. I cuddled her as she needs, and wondered who would do this for her now. Yes, she hugs a lot. She needs to. In common with most 'Downs,' she is a tactile person. Tenderness, and the kind of intimate care that would be lacking in this or any other home, however excellent, was what meant so much to her. Was I about to deprive her of all that was meaningful?

"Why don't you bring Mum to the kitchen for a cuppa?" a voice behind us suggested. A man around my own age had appeared and said he had put the kettle on. A more obviously genuine and caring person there could hardly have been, and drawing two chairs from the table, he then showed Minty where everything was kept. We both warmed to him immediately and he told her that if she had any odd jobs that needed doing then he was her man. She seized the initiative and asked him to show her how to get all the TV channels.

"No problem. That's what we'll do when Mum goes," he promised and I was grateful for his sensitivity in taking over those initial minutes when for the first time in her life I wouldn't be there. It all added to the feeling we had got it right after all.

I tried to get up to leave, and discovered my body was no longer obeying my brain. The final moment had come. It was the end of our life together.

"She's going to be fine," he whispered. "You're both tired. Go and land on family for a bit."

Oh if only family were there to be landed on, and in my longing I forgot the hostility her proposed move had created. Feebly I returned his smile. How could I say 'Night darling' without it sounding as if I were going to Australia, or leaving her in hospital? A nauseous pain tightened in my chest as my feet rooted more stubbornly to the floor. I couldn't imagine days without her.

Then came the bombshell. A resident I hadn't met, and very loudly handicapped, suddenly appeared and threw a heavy arm around Minty. "You coming to live here?" she asked indifferently. Taken aback, Minty jumped and then withdrew into herself. My heart sank. In checking every other imaginable detail, had I made a fundamental mistake in asking her to live with someone utterly incompatible? But she would surely have met her at one of the suppers or her stopover or on a daily basis at the Centre? Strange she hadn't mentioned her.

If we were making a mistake, it should have been in my power to stop it, but the venture had assumed a life and momentum of its own. Grace reappeared and said she had cooked supper and it seemed as if the moment she and the kindly Joe were on hand, Minty felt again the security they generated.

"Night Mum," she said, as she gave her hand to another. And at that moment I thought my heart would break. It was my hand she had held from being a baby; my hand she had gripped when feeling unsure or confused. And now, after over forty years, that hand was empty.

I was troubled by the amount of rich gravy poured over a piece of ham though it had been cooked according to the carer's taste. It was the first night, and by tomorrow she would doubtless have been given the diet suggestions I had handed into the office. She had seemed to make supper in no time at all and with no more ceremony than to put a knife and fork on the table. Would Minty miss the special table we always laid? Vase of flowers, pretty cloth etc. But our ways were not sacrosanct....

I was about to open the main door when the Deputy came out of the office. "Perhaps you'd let me have this back when you've had a moment to fill it in," she said, handing me a folded sheet of paper. Not trusting myself to speak, I nodded, pocketed it, and somehow my legs got as far as the door and into the car.

But I couldn't go home to a house made empty by the absence of someone so special and with whom my whole existence had been entwined since being told so many years ago, 'Your baby is going to need such special care.'

65

I did something rare for me and called on a friend without invitation or prior phone call. A friend who was also a 'soul mate.'

"Jeannie, I'm sorry but...."

She took one look at me and said, 'Take your coat off and sit down. I'm going to pour you a drink."

"I think I've got it wrong," I wept. "After all that checking, all those questions, I've got it wrong. What's the point of it being clean as a new pin and the staff so wonderfully kind if she doesn't like the people she lives with?"

Friend that she was she said quietly, "Maybe. And if you have, it can be reversed. But Minty likes it enough to want to try - very keen even. And you too were very sure about it. You're strung up right now: not the time to reverse decisions. Take things gently, one day at a time. The answer will come. Best for both of you if you don't visit tomorrow."

Months afterwards when she was home again, Minty showed me her diary entry for that first night.

After supper Emily shouted because she didn't want to wash up. Someone told her off. I went to Peter's lounge, and watched Emmerdale + Coronation Street and then he watched something he wanted so I went to my room. Got my things ready for next day. I hope I wake in time. I miss mum. Joe is nice and Grace. Emily is playing her music loud.

(And Next day) *I got up without a call. Breakfast was ready on the table and we just helped ourselves to cereals but the milk was cold. I put some in the microwave and it came over the top.*

I stayed with Jeannie until I'd pulled myself together. There were messages on the answerphone when I got home but I couldn't bring myself to respond to any of them. Falling onto the bed, my mind reeled from one question to another. Was she sleeping soundly or feeling anxious about the morrow? Would they sense that she might not ask for help even when she needed it? It had been the worst day of my life and would, I suspected, be the darkest night.

And in those hours, I knew I had not three, but four basic needs; warmth, food, shelter - and Minty. I had been born with three;

the last had developed as my love for her had intensified, as only a parent of another handicapped child would understand. So vulnerable in this cruel world, they evoke a depth of loving that forges an indestructible bond. Two lives become one as the carer thinks, plans and reacts for two. Nothing is arranged, no invitation accepted or issued, no appointments sought, or changes agreed to, without thinking in terms of the domino effect on a shared life.

Throwing my coat on the chair, I noticed the form the Deputy had given me, protruding from the pocket. Listlessly I unfolded it, then shocked and stultified, allowed it to fall from my grasp. I was to indicate funeral arrangements should they become appropriate.

Planning for her care beyond my own death had consumed all the strength I could muster today; planning for hers was beyond me.

CHAPTER EIGHT

I had a computer course the following day, and was grateful for the need to concentrate, though I absorbed little of what was taught. On the way home, and for the first time in my life I bought bread for one. A light so bright had gone out in my life, but on day two – though for me it might well have been day twenty - she was happy. And that being the case, I must be happy with, and for her, and put my trust in others to keep her so; start to make positive plans to change my own modus vivendi in tandem with hers. Truth was I had no idea how to begin, and certainly not the motivation.

A young man who had done our repairs for so many years that we had become friends, called in around noon to measure up for the wood needed to fix the pergola. I made him a coffee and suddenly he said, "I think there's a repair that's more urgent. Join me for a pub lunch?"

"Is it that obvious?"

"Only by the white face, black rings under your eyes, twitchy fingers, the weight loss...," he teased.. "Apart from that no one could tell. Come on. Get your coat."

We had shared so many in depth conversations over the years particularly when he lost daily access to his children. The cost to him of being deprived of such contact had been enormously destructive, and only years later as the girls became old enough to decide for themselves to see him regularly, did he look well again. But I saw at first hand how treacherously a troubled mind impacts on the physical.

Lunch, albeit a baguette, lasted the best part of two hours, during which I glanced at my watch several times.

"You don't need to any more," he said gently. "There's time for you now."

Time. A huge empty mass of it. And it stretched before me like a death sentence

* * *

Minty and I had agreed we would talk on the phone each evening around six-thirty, before the soaps began. I must call on the payphone that was just outside her room, and on which she could call me. Greg told me she was washing her hair and would call me back. So relieved was I that she had obviously not been watching the clock, that I made a sandwich and thrilled to the sound of the phone ten minutes later, but she was evidently not pressing the right button. I heard the receiver being replaced and dialled her immediately.

She was in good spirits and told me that 'a lady' had put up some decorations and I was glad that despite the last minute hiccups, she had moved at a time of busy Christmas activity. I asked what she'd had for supper and was told a fish parcel in parsley sauce in a plastic bag. Charley had 'cooked' it after he took it out of the packet.

"I like him," she enthused. "He's fun and we laughed a lot all the time." Her voice dropped, and she whispered confidentially, "But you know something Mum, they don't serve wine with the dinner here!"

We had lived on the Continent for enough years to cultivate the habit of a glass of vino with our evening meal - a routine we had continued on our return to England in the early seventies, and I hadn't thought to prepare her for the change.

"They probably don't sweetie," I laughed, thinking of the hole it would make in the 'sixteen pounds left over for living.' "But we'll have an extra glass of plonk at the weekend to make up."

She said "It's nice talking to you like this - just like we do at home isn't it. The phone is right outside my room so I'll always be here when you call. I love you best in the world. And you're still my mum on the phone aren't you?"

The lump in my throat was choking me. "I'll always be Mum wherever we are."

69

"Even in the night time?"

"All the time. Every single minute."

"I like that. I miss your cuddles."

I don't know why the receiver didn't break in half from the pressure I was putting on it.

"Oh Mum," she said suddenly. You owe Mrs. Quin some money. I went riding this afternoon at Centre."

"Weren't you given your five pounds before you left?" I asked and was assured it had been put in an envelope the night before. That was a good sign - they were organised re the daily needs I had listed. "So what went wrong? Did you lose it?"

"No, but Billy came without his money and couldn't go with his group to the other stables, so I cut my five pound note in half so we could both have a little time's ride."

Had they gone to the same venue, I daresay the problem could have been resolved, but in the event, the half notes were acceptable at neither!

It reminded me of the occasion when Mrs Thatcher had obviously enjoyed Mr Gorbechev's visit and news coverage had been given to the special relationship. A visitor who was intrigued as I put the requisite coins for Minty's activities into four separate envelopes, watched as I fished in my bag for change, and we had one of those charming snapshots of how random bits of information heard on television, had penetrated.

"Here," our visitor had offered, reaching into his pocket. "I've plenty. Glad to get rid of the weight."

Minty handed him a note in exchange for the coins. "Thank you," she said solemnly. "It's good to do business with you!"

We laughed about the shared note, and discussed another solution should the problem arise again. Such innocent concern for each other; the caring of instinct rather than intellect.

I could hear the signature tune for East Enders. "Does Peter watch it too?" I asked

"Yes he likes that."

Such relief that she wouldn't be sitting in her room alone.

"Bye now. Enjoy the Christmas lunch tomorrow!"

"I will. I've got my dress and jewels ready. I'm going to the Centre first then we'll all go to a special hotel. There'll be turkey and roast potatoes and Christmas pudding and mints....Oh my diet!"

"Diets are abandoned on special occasions," I said. "We all need treats now and then."

"We do, don't we. And I can be careful again afterwards."

"Before you go to bed, look inside the pocket of the case on the bottom of your wardrobe," I said. "You'll find a little bottle of perfume and something special in a tiny box."

She was excited at the mention of it. She loves dressing up for occasions, and even though the special meal was to be lunch, not dinner, she would attend in her cocktail dress and 'diamonds.'

And some of the misery lifted. Maybe it was going to work after all. I phoned Jeannie afterwards to tell her. Serene fount of wisdom that she was, she instructed quietly. "Good. Now go and get a proper night's sleep," though I hadn't mentioned I'd lain awake all the previous night. "Then one day at a time remember. Let life carry you along a little."

I told her of my intent to try to change my pattern of thinking to live our lives separately.

"Nothing so profound yet," I heard the soft tones. "You've only been two days apart."

Two days! Was that all it had been? It had felt like forever and I was totally without focus and purpose, aching that she should be happy and safe whilst fumbling in the dark for my own lost identity. Between the way things were now, and the way things used to be, was such a bleak echoing emptiness. I put the kettle on, not because I wanted coffee, but it was something automatic requiring no concentration; an insignificant procedure to help consume the empty hours ahead.

I who never in my life had enough hours in the day, was now pleading for them to fly until the weekend. I had hardly filled the cup when the phone rang. It was the Deputy.

"Something wrong?" I blurted and cursed myself for giving the impression I was less than calm.

71

"No, of course not. But you need to tell your surgery to give me Minty's prescription so that we can order hers with everyone else's on a monthly basis."

"Yes. I've already agreed with Mr. Brown that well before the current one runs out, I'll ask our surgery to fax the next prescription through to you so that the transfer will be smooth. Meanwhile I've given you the whole month's supply, less the ones she'll need at weekends."

"It makes sense for us to do it now that we're responsible for her."

Her choice of phrase gutted me. I had collected the routine monthly supply ahead of Minty's residency so that she would be well stocked. *And I wasn't dead yet.* Could I not be part of the equation too in this transition period? After only two days, I was incapable of staying on the periphery, let alone absenting myself altogether.

"Please don't ask me to," I was screaming silently. Did she really expect me to evaporate from my daughter's life after over forty years of caring for her every need? I sensed an efficient intent to absorb her into the system, into a routine pattern. But please let's do it humanely.

Had Minty moved on the 17th as first agreed, I would have collected her on Friday after her Christmas celebration, but having only been there since Wednesday - though Heaven knows there was no 'only' about it, I suggested (very level-headedly I thought in the circumstances) I should perhaps call for her on Saturday instead.

"If you think that's a better idea?" I asked the Deputy, shocked that she didn't nominate me for a medal for heroism, but she said only, "Of course, whatever is most convenient. Minty can come and go whenever she likes."

Convenience was the last thing on my mind. Had I been in charge, and Minty someone else's daughter, I would have suggested that my coming on Friday might prove disruptive to the settling in process, and Saturday, - the morning at least, - would provide a relaxed taste of what weekends were like at Greenlands. Was I imagining it, or was she taking it as read that the move was permanent whether or not she monitored the settling in process? I wished now that I had not deprived myself of such precious hours, but I'd already persuaded Minty it would help her adjust. But this was for management surely? Mrs. Quin hadn't seemed uncaring - far from it. Maybe one of those untroubled, confident people who 'go with the flow' to use the modern vernacular. It was too early to judge. She was most probably just being polite and helpful to me. And as she had said, freedom to come and go was part of the 'agreed policy.'

That evening I heard all about the hotel lunch. Some of her ex instructors had been there and she had had a wonderful time. She had been asked to dance, had come back with a present and had enjoyed 'smelling nice' all day.

"I'm glad I have two lovely homes now," she said, and sounded genuinely happy. "And would I please get her a new laundry basket as she didn't like the green plastic one provided, and would I ring Heather to make an appointment about her shakes." It didn't make sense - the happy bubbling, and yet she would not have asked to see Heather had she not been bothered by spasms.

It had been in our search, and willing to go anywhere or meet with anyone who might provide a solution that we were introduced to the homeopathic healer. How much she actually achieved I don't know. What I do know is that Minty felt better after a visit and had a lot of faith in her.

I was mystified that she had mentioned her today, having obviously enjoyed being with people she'd been so happy to see, for there was no mistaking the effervescence over the phone. Did she expect the night time to be different? And I recalled her question 'You're still my Mum at night-time?'

Spasms had begun quite suddenly after a 'relaxation session' at her Centre. The instructor had asked the group to imagine themselves by a stream, listen to the music that seemed to ripple, and then wander into a field of buttercups and feel the sun on their faces......... Evidently Minty fell deeply asleep and didn't wake when the music ended and the others had trundled off for a cup of tea. Perhaps the instructor became anxious; Minty only recalls hearing someone say, 'Come on luvvie, the others have all gone to tea break.'

If there is anything in the world she hates, it is to break the rules or fail to do what is expected of her. What would doubtless have been encouraging words to reassure the instructor she hadn't gone into hypnosis were interpreted by Minty as criticism. She was late for tea break! Aware of 'a big shake' in her neck whilst she was having her drink, she continued to be disturbed by involuntary muscle movement all that evening.

I watched through the night, concerned that intermittent spasms occurred even during sleep, and decided to seek medical advice as soon as possible. And over the years we have seen specialists, who whilst gaining a degree of relief through medication, have never established cause or cure. What is apparent is that the spasms are linked to anxiety and fatigue; hence I do everything possible to avoid both.

I had explained why it might be a good idea to stay at Greenlands until Saturday and to my relief she had been happy that she would see Jane who would be on weekend duty. Though the newest and youngest carer had been introduced as Minty's special person, she had seen very little of her in the three days she had been there. It seemed odd that her duties had not coincided with the arrival of the resident for whom she was to have personal care, for it would surely have been a simple matter to juggle the staff roster given the rarity of having new entrants.

Sadly the Saturday was not quite as she had hoped, and yet maybe no bad thing that she saw the reality of the situation. Knowing Jane was her special carer she had imagined she would be spending quality time with her. But of course other residents also needed time and attention. Not having previously met them, it was only now that I was able to appreciate that some had significantly greater need. I had also learned that the more attractive lounge in which I had had most of my meetings with the Manager, was unofficially seen as being theirs, though at no time would either be barred to whoever wanted to use them.

The house appeared to divide naturally, and generally meals were eaten in the two separate dining room/kitchens, but on special occasions there was room for all to gather around one table in either. The whole house was most pleasantly appointed and scrupulously clean and though residents seemed to use the lounge nearest to their own rooms, there appeared to be no hard and fast rule.

She called me later to say that Jane wouldn't be coming on duty until after lunch on Saturday and would stay on duty over Christmas. There were two issues at stake here I recognised, and to face the second I'd need to call on a last reserve of courage.

"So would you prefer me to collect you about five thirty instead of mid morning? That way you can spend time with Jane before I come." I paused and then said, "And if you'd rather spend Christmas there, that's fine." Courage was paper-thin and almost instantly began to desert me, and I struggled to add, "Maybe you could invite me to Christmas lunch? That would be very special."

My God, I deserved an Oscar.

"I want Christmas at home with you," was her reply.

Mightily relieved that no public performance would be called for, the part of me still managed by my head saw it as a missed opportunity to consolidate the settling in process.

I arrived on Saturday, complete with laundry basket. En route to Minty's room I saw Grace in the office because she kept the door wide open so that anyone needing her could see immediately where she was - an enormous brownie point for her, as far as I was concerned.

"You OK?" she asked as I passed.

"I'm working on it."

"I'm here for you too you know."

She, like the hospice staff who had nursed my husband, had recognised that in any profound change to lives there is more than one 'patient.' For me, such sensitivity rocketed to the top of the qualification criteria. Emotion was too close to the surface. I smiled my thanks and she promised she'd look out for my girl.

"We enjoy having her," she called. "She's lovely." She came into the corridor and added. "And it's cutting you up isn't it?"

I told her that in trying to protect the future, I hoped fervently that I'd done the right thing. The problem was that 'the future' now seemed a million miles away, and here was this interminable stretch of greyness called the 'present.'

"When she's settled in you'll start to build a life of your own," she said.

"She *is* my life. I've lived it with her since her birth. I don't know of another," I replied in defiance of the implication that my daughter was an imposition.

That was unfair of me for I was well aware of the danger of having only one time consuming focus; that it would be healthier if we could both live fuller lives. Indeed since retirement from a profession of total engagement with others, the lack of compatible human contact needed to be addressed, for I must refuse many invitations to join with friends who were now enjoying the second 'playtime' of their lives. Unrestricted by timetables, they could delay the return home or change plans spontaneously.

For over forty years all my strength had gone on protecting her, making sure she was fulfilled and happy. Now I was being asked to be strong and do exactly the opposite; to let her go. But all I could feel was the strength of my own weakness and I desperately needed help. Not the sort of thing one admitted.

Minty was packed and ready. She and Jane exchanged affectionate farewells, and wished 'Happy Christmas - see you soon.' That they liked each other was undeniable. We called at the office to deposit Christmas cards and chocolates and Minty hugged Grace who had obviously spent time with her.

"I like Grace. She's very cuddlable. She's the apple of my side!"

I was glad that no political correctness had impeded Grace, for hugs were as essential to Minty as food and sleep. And thank goodness it was self evident she was the apple of her eye rather than the thorn in her side! Not only was there a complete lack of lateral thinking, she understands only the literal, having immense difficulty with clichés and idioms, and merely repeats those she has heard someone else say to effect, with only an outside chance of their being in context.

"Alright if we come back after Boxing Day?" I asked. Saturday was already almost over and Christmas Eve the day after tomorrow. Such a brief time would fly past.

"Sounds like a very good idea," Grace smiled.

"When will you be on duty?" Minty asked her.

"Most of the time it's beginning to look like! I'm doing some filling in. You have a super Christmas now."

"I will. I always have nice Christmas with Mum – lots of years now. Bye Grace. Oh and please give my *cobliments* of the season to Mr. Brown when he comes," she added formally.

Had she asked about rosters because she was glad when Grace was on duty or because there was someone with whom she wasn't so comfortable? We would chat casually in the days we had together and I could pick up clues. Maybe I'd need to explain that in every walk of life people have their favourites but favourites would become worn out if they didn't get a break now and then.

Enough that it was Christmas and we were together again. The roads were icy but I would have gone over glaciers to collect her. Joy oozed from every pore and I wanted to shout out to the world that my girl was coming home again. I squeezed her hand but one glance told me she had fallen asleep. It was almost immediate. I pulled over towards the kerb and gently drew to a halt.

"Why have you stopped?" she asked.

"I thought you were ill."

"No just tired. I didn't get a nap today 'cos I waited for Jane coming. I will at home. Love you Mum."

It felt like a 'goodbye' and an icy fear gripped as the memory of my mother on the return journey from the market flashed before me. Then was I imagining it or did she come into the house only tentatively? She paused by the tree we had decorated two weeks earlier. "All green and gold," she whispered. "And more presents have come. It's Christmas time. Just us and Christmas."

"Do you want company – I'll ask....."

"No." she stopped me in my tracks. "Just you and me like always. Christmas eve supper, and carols and opening presents and a big fire and lighting the pudding and all the things we do."

Then the tears came - hers and mine - and the fiercest embrace made a good job of mixing them up.

"It was a big step sweetie, wasn't it? But you did it."

"And I do like it. But I wanted Christmas with you. It's special." She looked at me for a few seconds and then said, "And I know you'll have to die one day like Nan but not yet and now it's Christmas like always."

My arms enclosed her and I didn't know how I would ever let her go again. I didn't want to be away from her for a single minute. And yet there was a sense we had crossed a Rubicon - as if there was something more out there than home. She hadn't said 'Oh it's good to be home' the way she does after a holiday, but rather 'I wanted to be with you for Christmas.'

We sat by the tree for some time, both knowing that something was different. My girl had moved on, and there was no going back even if it didn't work out. Maybe it was because she had tasted independence, enjoyed new company, the stimulus of people coming and going. Yet she didn't crave company for Christmas and on going to her room just checked that everything was exactly as she had left it.

The vibes were confusing.

CHAPTER NINE

I expected her to sleep in late on Sunday, but she came down for breakfast at nine, ate her cornflakes and said, "You're such a marvellous cook."
I whispered my thanks to Mr Kelloggs and perhaps should have read something into her comment but was too amused by the compliment to register the innuendo. She said again that she liked Greenlands, though remarked again how noisy Emily was and wished she wasn't, and described staff who were particularly nice, giving an opportunity to check if there was anyone with whom she had a problem.

"Hugh's really lovely. Very shy and kind. Charley's fun and jokey and makes me laugh. Joe does lots for us. He mends stuff and fixes lights and things. Grace talks to me a lot and Jane is really nice and Sarah and Mr. Brown. I don't know Mrs. Quin much. She's in the office a lot and does all the papers. That's all the people I know yet."
Nothing significant there except I would have thought the Deputy would want to get to know the newest of her residents as part of the job.

We had breakfast and the cloud lifted because we had each recognised there were now two homes and that both could be pleasurable. It seemed she was already adjusting whilst her mother hadn't even begun. Later in the morning I breezed into her room as always and put some clean clothes on her chair for her to organise as she wished, and was halted when she said, "Oh Mum you must remember to knock at my door. It's a house rule! After all I might be getting changed."
I wondered how many more house rules I didn't know I had, would surface!

79

It had been arranged since before Minty left home for Eddy, her friend for twenty years now, to come for Sunday lunch with a Christmas flavour. I had feared she would by then have got a taste for more company than just me and I didn't want it to seem flat when she returned. Long afterwards, I could appreciate that she hadn't really been away the eternity it had seemed, and wouldn't have had time to develop a strong sense of the differences in four days.

They were easy in each other's company and sat together after lunch like an old married couple. When I suggested a game of dominoes I think they played more to please me than themselves. Eddy soon returned to the armchair, the tendency to sit quietly and absorb the television being no different from what had begun a year or so ago. I looked at them both - such good friends since childhood, and saw two heads with more than a few grey hairs between them, placidly nodding off. They made no demands on each other to stay awake due being guest and hostess. They were who they were, and content to be so. All the turmoil was in me.

On Christmas Eve we went for the now traditional lunch to our favourite country pub, a beautiful Elizabethan inn whose proprietors had become friends. We sat at 'our' table and savouring the superbly cooked meal to the full, at last I felt calm. Over coffee Margaret took time from the kitchen to chat and Minty told her of developments. When I went to the bar to settle the bill, Alan talked to me almost like a brother, not bothering with pleasantries or clichés, recognising we had only a few minutes before Minty joined us. He knew that the step we had taken had been done in the interests of protecting her future and didn't judge or offer opinion, only advised to open up my own world when I'd got used to new situation

"Though I think that's going to be harder for you than you imagine," he said, insisting we had a drink with them. But I'd already had a large wine and must now drive home. He didn't pressure, but as we got our coats and said goodbye to all the familiar faces, he rounded the bar and presented Minty with a bottle of Piesporter, making her feel like a celebrity. He told her she was wonderful and kissed us both. I wanted to hang onto such genuine sentiment; solitude has such a dearth of it. And there was more than one smile from the 'regulars' as she was heard telling him he was a 'marble.'

"We think you're *marbelous* too!" he joked. "Have a good Christmas now."

"We will," she responded with such confidence that my heart leapt. "We always have nice Christmas."

So far so good. At least for Christmas I was enough for her. One day at a time, Jeannie had counselled.

But on Christmas morning she wondered how Jane was getting on. This was crunch time; a forcible reminder that her world had broadened. Faking cheerfulness, I suggested driving her over with a box of mince pies and goodies. Across my consciousness flew the idea that they would no doubt absorb one extra for lunch but two would be an imposition, and driving back to an empty house after all had seemed to be going so well, would be doubly harrowing. But if that's what was called for, so be it. And I wouldn't even try to go through the motions of Christmas, but spend the day writing; just finding a way to get through it.

"No Mum," she insisted. But she would phone to wish Jane a Happy Christmas, because she wasn't with *her* Mum for Christmas and would be missing her. It was Charley, whom I hadn't yet met, who answered her call.

"Minty are you sure?" I whispered whilst she still held the receiver. "It would only take half an hour."

"Yes." And I thought it was an answer to my question. But she was talking to Charley. "Yes I'm having a lovely Christmas and we've got a turkey that's very big. You could all come over here if you like. You'd be very welcome. We'd just need to peel a few extra 'vegables' and potatoes. Wouldn't take a minute. And we've got a pudding......"

My mind reeled. In seconds I had gone from a solo, non-existent Christmas to wondering how to inflate a moderate size turkey that would satisfy a crowd. Any turkey is too big for two, but this would be the challenge of the decade. I breathed a sigh of relief as she replaced the receiver.

"They're fine," she announced. "I just wanted to make sure they weren't lonely. They're going to have their dinner soon. Shall we open the presents now?"

I nodded, smiled, and to myself added, "As long as that's the last hurdle I'm to jump this morning!"

She looked at the colourful parcels under the tree and then paused. "We usually open Nan's first and then phone her, don't we?" I could sustain the performance no longer. What a year it had been.

"Miss Nan, she whispered. "Missed you too Mum." And at that moment I knew I had done nothing less than die a little in her absence.

We did eventually open the gifts, rang family, piled more logs on the fire and took time to look more closely at all the cards. As always, one depicted the 'perfect' Victorian Christmas - a family in affluent surroundings and a maid bringing in an enormous turkey. Minty's gaze was fixed by it for some moments and then inspired, she said enthusiastically, "Let's dress up for dinner too, in long dresses to go with the best cutlery and candles."

"Fine - just as soon as we've got everything in the oven. Not sure I can find a tiara for you though."

"That's alright. I've got my diamonds."

We ate heartily, generously brandied and lit the pudding, and after the Queen's speech Minty scanned the Radio Times, decided there was nothing worth her attention for a couple of hours so it was a good time for a nap. Alone in the kitchen I felt more than a little ridiculous stacking the dishwasher whilst resplendent in long dress and rubber gloves!

I took my coffee into the lounge and sat by the fire, watching the flames and thinking. Only one more day and she would be leaving again. Was this what life was to be from now on - seesawing between meeting and being torn apart? She would go back for four days and then come home again for New Year. At least that was what had been assumed. Now the arrangement seemed needlessly unsettling and I wondered how she would feel about staying home a day or two longer and then returning to spend New Year's Eve with her new companions. That way the two periods would be less fractured for her. Time enough to raise the idea tomorrow; nothing must spoil today. She was sleeping a long time. Or maybe I was just conscious of the limited time we had and didn't want to waste one moment.

Minty always, but always, prepares herself for the day ahead; what clothes to wear, what she was likely to need, all to hand. Sure enough at breakfast on Boxing Day she said, "Aren't the days going quickly? Now I'll have to get my things ready and then bring them home again and then pack again. I think I'll ring them up and say it's too rushed."

Blandly, so as not to pressure her one way or the other, I put my idea to her. She received it decisively as if it were obvious commonsense.

"I'll do that. When is New Years?"

"Next Tuesday. Always the same day as Christmas."

We settled for returning on Sunday morning because lunch was the main meal on Sundays, and a pretty spectacular one by all accounts. I hoped that this way she could share in the preparations for New Year's Eve supper. We rang to check that such an arrangement was acceptable and one they would be happy with, and again I was puzzled.

"Minty must come and go as she pleased. She could stay home for the whole period if she wished," the Deputy said agreeably.

So after being there for only four days it was fine to stay home for two weeks. Surely such a timetable was hardly conducive to settling in. And though I longed for her to do just that, I knew it was not in her best interests. It was play-acting time again, for me at any rate. Minty decided to take two more certificates for her new room.

"I don't think they know yet how qualified I am," she said, and plumped for taking her 'Basics of Babysitting theory', and 'Sound, Rhythm and Music' certificates.

I didn't imagine there would be much call for help with baby-sitting so I asked if she wouldn't rather take her swimming or 'Life Skills' awards.

"No I've already got my trophies and I had to have help with the Life Skills. It says on it, look. The lady said I could say the answers 'cos I couldn't write them."

As ever, at her own level, only perfection would do!

The mention of swimming made me realise that I hadn't told her I had chanced to see Kevin recently. He had included her in the many swimming galas he had organised for the handicapped and was one of her all time favourites.

"I expect he'll be looking forward to a special birthday too this year," I said.

"Will he?"

"Yes. Don't you remember, except for one day he's the same age." She nodded thoughtfully, and then, "Um. He used to be. But I don't know if he still is."

This gem of logic would be lost on 'normality', but I recognised that because she hadn't seen him for two or three years and therefore hadn't been on the receiving end of his banter when birthdays *had* occurred, she assumed that such events had bypassed him!

We got to Greenlands in good time for lunch. Greg, another member of staff I hadn't yet spoken with, welcomed her back. Instinctively I liked and trusted him; sensitive and straightforward was my first impression. Minty squeezed my hand, gave me a hug, told me that Christmas had been special and that she would unpack with Jane.

Jane had laid a table for everyone in Dining Room One, but Robert preferred eating in Dining Two in his half of the house, and immediately Minty said she would join him. I left them together with an impressive Sunday roast and more calories than I dared think about - but anything to help the settling in process. She had a new world, and as long as I was within reach, appeared to be enjoying it. I must suppress my yearning ache and do nothing to detract from that enjoyment.

I left a note in the office saying she'd had a new CD Player for Christmas and perhaps she could have help until she was used to it. She was due for a blood test that could be done any time in January ready for her day-stay in hospital the next month, and the relevant form was enclosed. I hoped it was possible to avoid Wednesdays so that she didn't miss the college course that she enjoyed so much. In February someone would need to stay with her for the whole day and unless it was a problem, I would like to do that. For two days prior to admission, her diet had to be very strictly monitored and I would provide them with written details nearer the time.

I also asked if there would be any objection to my making some curtains that would complement the new colour scheme in her room. It seemed such a lot of requests and information, for which I apologised, but nevertheless hospital details were best written down so there could be no misunderstanding.

There was absolutely no response or reaction to the note, so I put the curtains on hold for a while. Maybe they'd felt affronted that I'd asked.

I woke feeling less anxious; relieved Minty had gone off with Jane so serenely the day before, and was working on my book when she phoned. She had had a bath and Grace had weighed her and she had lost four pounds!! My mind flew to the two substantial Yorkshire puddings and crispy roast potatoes of yesterday. Perhaps soon they would be able to look at the requests re her diet that had been agreed. I hoped so. It shouldn't cause any extra work to substitute a couple of boiled potatoes.

"That's wonderful," I enthused. "Tell Grace to let me know where she bought her magic scales!"

"I'll ask her," she said absolutely seriously. "They're really good ones Mum. We should get some."

Robert had gone home she told me, but Peter was here. It was a good night on television and they could watch a lot together. "Watching tele is better than talking," she said, "cos Peter speaks so softly I can't hear him." There was a pause and then, "What are you going to do tomorrow?"

I told her of my intention to take a gift to someone who had gone out of her way to find some information I needed. "You remember," I said. "We met her in town when we were shopping for the things you needed for your room – she was just finishing a coffee at the next table when we stopped for a break."

"I remember," she said thoughtfully. "The *posh and pisticated* lady in the furry hat."
Oops! Though unaware, she had corrupted a complimentary adjective and substituted one of her own making that was not a totally inaccurate description of my new acquaintance.

We continued our chat and I was content to hear that Grace was on duty 'and nice, and she was happy.'
"So, perhaps I won't call you this evening?"
"Yes please call me. Half past six like always?"
But she called me earlier at 6.20,
"Everything alright?" I asked, deliberately keeping my voice light and cheerful.
"Yes. I just wanted to hear you - and tell you we've had a New Year's Eve supper - special with punch. It was lovely."

So she likes it still, but needs to know we are in contact. I think I can live with that, I decided. But what a chasm I now inhabited. I wrote late into the night in an effort to stop thinking about her, but to no avail. Wondering what she was doing, what was going through her mind, was superimposed on all that I did. And why hadn't she waited for me to phone as agreed; she could have told me then about the supper. Or had someone suggested it? And even if they had, she had sounded genuine if not excited. Was I looking for problems where none existed?

Later in the year, she showed me her diary entry for that day:

'We had special New Year supper but it was quick over and I come back to my room and cried. It wasn't the same without mum. We would have all eve together and not just the little time. We would bop around the kitchen until mum was puffed out and then play 'Give me a Clue' and watch tele together and have special coffee in pretty cups. I want to go back home and do all the special things for New Year that we do. I want some more years together. I can come here if Mum dies. Grace has to help everyone so we only talk sometimes. She is nice lady and ask me if I joyed it and I said yes thank you and she say tell mum and make mum happy. I did, but I didn't really. But

86

I couldn't hurt Grace's feelings. That's not nice and I want mum be happy. We love each other so much.'

Had I seen the diary on the day it was written would my reaction have been rational? Was it not an entry much as would have been written by a 'normal' girl missing home for the first time? But Minty wasn't 'normal' in the accepted sense. And she hadn't gone to college with a future career in mind that depended on her seeing the course through. But as yet the diary was closed to me.

On January 1st, I rang her, as all the family members. An hour later she rang to wish *me* Happy New Year!

"Ring again at the evening like always," she urged, and of course I promised.

I mused on her words 'like always'. So for her too, the two weeks apart had felt long enough to feel 'always'. The hours crawled and when I phoned all seemed well. Charley and Hugh were on duty and she liked them both enormously. Joe had cooked supper and the two younger fellows had sat down with the residents, which made a world of difference. She asked me to get blank tapes and hooks for more pictures, so she must be feeling secure.

I reflected on her asking me to bring things in as though I were an outside contact and she in hospital. I must mention it to staff tomorrow to see if it was possible for her to go out with one of them to shop. I really needed to know it would happen if I were no longer around. Could staff in fact leave the premises to go out with one when there were others, even more handicapped, to be cared for? Another question I should have asked earlier. I had asked a million, yet still there were more I had missed.

Meanwhile the diary she was using as a friend contained this entry for New Year's Day.

Nobody came to say goodnight hug like mum. I got undressed and went to bed. I didn't want to stay up to see the new year in. It was hot in my room and I didn't like open my window because the garden was outside, so I took my top off and pushed the sheets down. The night lady came in and she knocked my door when my door was wide

open because I like to see the corridor light. I woke up and she said put your top on. Someone might see you.
Now I had a spasm. I kept shaking all night. I couldn't go back to sleep. I wanted mum so much.

On January Thursday 2nd she didn't call. Was this a good sign or was she feeling down and not wanting to worry me? That would be like her. And I needed so much to know. Promptly at six thirty I called, and she seemed less bubbly and said she had had a bad night after watching distressing soaps, but I wasn't persuaded. Usually if she found a programme disquieting she promptly switched it off. She said she was very happy, but not so convincingly, and asked if we could celebrate at the weekend and have candlelight supper. When I asked what we were going to celebrate especially, she said, "Being together for Saturday night. I can lay a pretty table and make it look special. I'll need a red candle – are they still in the kitchen cupboard?"

It was as if she feared that something as insignificant as a candle might not be in a familiar place. I was screwed up again and fought such a battle with myself not to fetch her home. It was good that Grace was on duty. Minty says she loves her to bits but I think maybe Grace encourages her to phone me with happy news so that I won't worry; and I had no doubt whatsoever that it was for the kindest of motives for whenever we chanced upon each other she gave the impression she was indeed there for both of us.

CHAPTER TEN

Minty had taken Thursdays off from the Training Centre for some years now 'to be housekeeper.' A long time ago it had been thought she could hold down a simple job but finding a placement had proved impossible and her manager had asked if I would be agreeable to her working at home, completely unaided. My school was some three miles away and in an emergency I could be back within minutes, and so I complied. I arranged for neighbours to 'happen to drop by' and for her to telephone my secretary at lunch times - ostensibly to leave a message telling me the post had come, but realistically to know all was well. And it had worked beautifully. Older neighbours enjoyed dropping by for a chat, coffee and cake, and she loved playing hostess. Hence I wondered how she would spend her Thursdays now.

"Shall we go shopping and out for coffee - you and me?" she asked. "You're retired now, so we could."

Again I thought that in her best interests there would be an objection, albeit gently made; that not going to the Centre would provide a golden opportunity for her to become more closely acquainted with staff by helping in the office or kitchen. And once more when I rang the Deputy to ask her advice she reiterated I was welcome to take my daughter out whenever we wished, that coming and going as she pleased was her 'right'.

"I thought perhaps you might want her to be with you and the staff," I said lamely and was told that equally Minty was more than welcome to stay if she preferred for staff were on site round the clock, but there was no mention of any bonding activity or shopping. And yet again I imagined what would happen if I had died, with no family living near. Thursdays would seem interminably long and tedious. After I had given her all the openings I could think of to advise me not to go, I said I'd be there at ten thirty.

Minty was withdrawn and said she had told staff she might not go to the Day Nursery tomorrow as she was tired - again a decision that had been accepted facilely. 'Her right to decide.' I was intrigued she hadn't been encouraged to keep up her routine, but then I'd been surprised when I hadn't been discouraged from taking her shopping given that she was due to come home next day, and decided that political correctness decreed that 'the client's wishes must be respected.'

But expressed wishes are not always the real ones. And certainly not in Minty's case. Her reply was invariably what she thought was expected, or people wanted to hear, or what she thought would make them happy. Did no-one scratch beneath such a fragile surface? It was crucial that they did. Had I been able to address the issue rationally and with any degree of calm, I would have accepted that it was early days yet and in time they would get to know her. But I was acting on instinct alone. And in any case, instinct is often as accurate as reason.

It took only minutes over coffee to realise she didn't want to go because she was worried about the 'different' arrangements for taking her, i.e. not me. She brightened after I said we would talk to staff and make certain all would be well, and that I would be waiting for her at the end of the session. So when we returned at lunchtime, she told the Deputy she had 'had a different think.'

"Shall we do it again next week Mum? It was fun. And I can make my own sandwich now when you go."

She was enjoying her new independence and yet needed to ascertain I would visit again next Thursday to spend time with her. I was getting such confusing messages and the uncertainty was gnawing away at me.

With hindsight I could say it was too soon to know, but every day assumed the longevity of a month. I must give it time according to what the calendar and not my heart told me. Maybe, just maybe, the days that had been routine for us in the past, could become special, special enough to outweigh the missing of each other on all the others.

I supposed I ought to make plans to go out for an evening. This was the freedom that well-meaning friends had urged for so long. 'Think what you could do with time for yourself,' they had encouraged. 'You've never gone anywhere without constantly looking at your watch.'

But freedom for what? I must be on my guard. If not careful, freedom could, in my present state mean not having a reason to get up in the morning, impelled by sheer inertia not to leave the house.

Next day I was waiting at the Day Nursery as promised and a happy passenger climbed in beside me.

"Good session?"

"Yes. And I made up with Peter before he went to Centre this morning."

"I didn't know you'd had a disagreement!"

"He was annoyed I had a day off yesterday and said I should have gone to Centre like him. But he's all right now."

So it wasn't disenchantment with the Home that had made her low yesterday. The problem had been identified. Such a relief. The emotional see-saw shot me skywards again.

"I see. And how did he feel about today?"

"All right. *He* wouldn't like to work with little children. And guess what, nice Hugh drove me to work. I like him a lot."

"So do I. He's a treasure, but very shy. I hope you got him to talk."

"We talked all the way. And he knows a different way to the Nursery - not as long as our way."

I smiled. Given she now lived much nearer to her job and that Hugh would have approached it from entirely the opposite direction, it was hardly surprising he had taken a different route!

"I'm glad you had such a good driver. You'll have to be patient with me if I take my usual long way home."

"I don't mind. And I'll always be patient with you. And maybe Hugh will come and drive *you* somewhere one day! He can *govergate* you so you don't get lost."

Shy as he was I didn't imagine the poor chap had aspirations to be a toy boy!

* * *

It was Saturday. We had leisurely breakfast and later, on a bright, sharply cold morning, drove to the 'Ferryboat Inn' for a sandwich lunch beside a roaring fire. The day was so precious because it was now part of something that would end. I found myself treasuring every moment I was with her, but I couldn't deny she had enjoyed new faces. And on Sunday she elected to return again in time for Sunday lunch. I met with Sarah, and talked with Charley, two impressively kind members of staff. I couldn't ask for better.

But I noted poor Emily's behaviour troubled Minty. Often noisy and emotional, and seemingly without family, she needed very special care. She wasn't always easy for the others to warm to, but obviously lonely and I felt so sorry for her. But she was Minty's only female companion apart from staff, and that did concern me, especially as the stated aims of the Home included 'a peaceful atmosphere,' in addition to 'the opportunity to learn new skills.'

However, as long as my girl hadn't mentioned the lack of a compatible friend, I mustn't put ideas in her head. Currently she had reservations about two of the carers she had met so far, and it was possible the situation could be resolved. She liked all the others immensely. We watched some news clips for awhile in her room; amusing, memorable and significant events that had shaped the previous year, and suddenly she asked, "What's the Queen doing to that man?"

"She's making him a knight," I explained. "He's a very talented sportsman, and won a gold medal for England. So now she's rewarding him."

"So he's famous now?"

"That's right."

She became reflective, and then, "So now you've had a book published will I be famous too? When will I be *damed?*"

A logical, if incorrect use of our language, and a reminder, if any were needed, of the interjections I used to enjoy daily!

"I don't think the book is important enough to make anybody famous. It's not as if it has been made into a film or anything....."

"So that's what you can do next week when I'm away – get it made into a film and sew a lovely ball dress for me to go and see the Queen. *And* I'll buy some dark glasses. All famous people wear them."

But on Monday rather more mundane matters needed my attention. I called at the surgery to tell them of the changed arrangements for future prescriptions and asked that the next month's supply be faxed to Greenlands so that Minty's could be collected with those of the other residents.

"It's already been done," the receptionist told me. "We had a call asking for the pills to be redirected now that she is living away."

I was annoyed and upset. I felt my promise had not only been ignored but that they considered I was not to be trusted; one of those irritating mothers who couldn't let go. On Thursday I would have to make it clear I hadn't appreciated the lack of courtesy. I was still very much alive, still her parent wanting to work in tandem for a smooth transition and a simple phone call would have made such a difference. At the same time I could have confirmed that what had been promised would be done.

But of course my initial agreement had been with the Manager whom at the time I had thought to be in charge of the day-to-day running of the home. Nevertheless I had acquainted Mrs. Quin of that agreement. It didn't excuse the action but there might be a simple explanation. I must stay calm; emotion would be counter productive and diminish me as a rational person with whom to deal. Maybe she preferred not having to deal with parents, especially ones disinclined to fit into 'systems'?

I determined to start coping with my 'new' life. I wrote a whole chapter next morning - then promptly tore it up before lunch. In the evening I went up to a London theatre; it must have been a good production by virtue of such an excellent cast yet I had no idea afterwards what it had been about. Would I ever be able to concentrate properly again? I must make more of an effort tomorrow. But tomorrow was my mammogram. I'd almost forgotten.

Despairing that I'd never actually get my resolve into gear, I was just leaving for the clinic when Minty, clearly distressed, phoned from the Centre.

"Mum, I've been overdosed!"

"Tell me what's happened."

Before I left this morning Mrs. Quin gave me three clobazam. She said I must take them."

"All at once? And in the morning?"

My mind went into overdrive, the priority being to assure her she was in no danger, and then to deal with the situation. She had obviously endured this fear all morning and the hours must have seemed interminable.

"Sweetie, you'll feel very relaxed and calm, but you're in no danger. Just find a place to sit quietly and you'll be absolutely fine. I'll phone your instructors and tell them what's happened and then I'll get on to Greenlands."

I wanted to ask her why she wasn't administering her own medication as had been agreed, but needed, at this moment, to direct her mind away from that particular territory.

"We'll sort it all out, I promise. I'll come now."

"No. You said I not die. We go bowling this afternoon."

"Of course, Tuesday's your special day, isn't it?"

So assurance had been all that was needed; to go and see her, much as I longed to, would suggest to her that there was something to worry about. In fact the pills were fairly innocuous but that wasn't the point, and I must alert staff as to the correct dosage I had written down for them. Until four o'clock she would be at her Centre and in no danger of being given any further medication.

I phoned to speak with the member of staff in question, but of course she had been on night duty and had now gone home. I explained the serious nature of my call, and insisted that everyone be ultra vigilant re further medication, which of course shouldn't have been necessary given that she had her own supplies in her room.

The reaction from Greg was tentative. "Have a word with Mrs. Quin," he said, and I sensed he would not wish to confront someone of senior rank. "I'm sure there'll be an explanation."

94

"I'd very much like to," I said. Perhaps you can tell me when she'll be back." There was a pause and a shuffling of paper.

"Not until Thursday."

Exasperated I said, "Please tell her that I must speak with her as soon as she returns. Meanwhile I'm coming now to bring a letter that must be given to Mr. Brown the moment he arrives."

I checked the letter again. Best to avoid antagonism or we would end up on opposite sides of the fence and confrontation would yield little. In essence I had asked them to refer to the medication details I had provided on the first day, told of the distress caused, and uncompromisingly said that in no circumstances must she ever again be given three pills together. The medication was to stem the effects of spasms over a twenty-four hour period.

I reiterated that our GP agreed it would be a retrograde step for her to be dosed as if she were a patient in hospital and that together we had spent many months training her to recognise her symptoms and to know when the pills would act to best effect. I had been perfectly happy with the suggestion she have a lockable box in her room for the safety of others, but reminded of the agreement that she should deal with her own medication.

I deposited the letter, marked 'urgent' in the office. Hugh was on duty and looked puzzled. "But Minty has her own pills. Just a minute, I'll go and check. Greg's preparing medication now."

I went to Minty's room just as she arrived back from her Centre and looked in the box she kept in her bedside cabinet. The packets had been removed and had been replaced by a day's quota. They were in her draw for her to administer as agreed but she was unable to see the tiny print on the foil backs and had no idea which were which, for not only were they of similar size but ALL WERE WHITE!

"She can look after her own medication as long as pills remain in packets," I said, and could tell from their expressions they were equally bewildered, and sympathetic to the fact of Minty's eyesight being quite unable to cope with the pills as they were.

"Everyone else is given medication by the carer on duty," Greg tried to soothe. "Perhaps it was felt necessary to deal with Minty's in the same way."

"And the fact it was contrary to the agreement I had with Mr. Brown?" I knew I was overwrought and fought to keep control.

They had picked up my notion of a possible discrepancy between two senior members and Greg said gently, "Mr. Brown will be here in the morning if you want to talk with him."

"And meanwhile?"

"Will you trust me to read the names of the pills to Minty? I'll separate the clobazam from those that must be taken when she wakes."

He was a reliable man and a sensitive one and I did indeed trust him. I was sorry they were on the receiving end of my agitation whilst not being responsible for it, and would return in the morning. I chatted with Minty until it was time for her supper, then driving home, my head churned through the day's events. This time I was able to reassure her. But what if I hadn't been around? It was, after all, for the time after my own death that I was trying to make arrangements. Constant resurfacing of the same question. The most important one.

* * *

"I'm sure Mrs. Quin will have been acting in everyone's best interest," Mr. Brown placated when I arrived early.

"Including my daughter's? By giving her the wrong dose at the wrong time? I hardly think so."

"I'm sorry, but you must appreciate Mrs. Quin has overall responsibility for Greenlands and I support her decisions."

At that moment it seemed that not only the goalposts, but the very ground was moving from beneath me.

"But we had an agreement, you and I - an agreement that was crucial to Minty's coming here. And that was with you as Manager. I had no idea you were not in daily charge, nor did I have reason to think otherwise. At no time was the Deputy mentioned, or that you didn't have the final say."

I paused, trying to keep a grip on my thinking. "I'd like to come and see you both together - something I should have done

96

months ago - if only I'd known then of the system, or indeed of Mrs. Quin's existence. I understand she'll be back tomorrow?"

"Of course. We'll both be here from mid morning onwards."

I recognised that not a great deal more would be achieved until then. Changing the emphasis, he told me that soon they would be appointing a new member of staff, and to represent the residents perhaps Minty would like to sit on the interviewing panel? He was sure she would be an asset and asked if I was happy for him to put the suggestion to her. Having heard now how he had 'met' her at the Centre and had learned from staff that we had been looking at the possibility of her trying to live away from home, I could see that on her own level she had been head-hunted!

It was indicative of the man's character that he acquainted me with this suggestion in the easy manner in which we had discussed her welfare prior to her residency and though frustrated by what I could only interpret as a refusal to assert himself on the medication issue, I was grateful to be involved again. Why couldn't the transfer of pharmacy have been discussed in the same trusting manner?

* * *

Evidently a member of staff phoned in sick next day, so there was no-one available to take Minty to her job. It was a pity it should have happened on the first occasion but it would have been the same if she or I had been sick. I accepted, and understood the situation, for if there were going to be teething problems it would be now, and this was an understandable one. Not needing to be on the other side of town by midday would give me longer to talk about the pills. It had turned out for the best.

Both were welcoming in a most friendly way and I was amazed at how calm and untroubled Mrs. Quin appeared, given what could have been the seriousness of my complaint. She was certainly not on the defensive, and seemed unaffected by my letter, the content of which I repeated. There was an apparent unawareness of the damage done, or understanding of the fear that had resulted in Minty phoning me from her Centre. Was it insensitivity or did she genuinely believe I was making a mountain out of a molehill?

Mrs. Quin smiled serenely, and said there really wasn't a problem. She produced the packet supplied by the 'new' chemist, and sure enough the label read '3 at night.'

She had taken the wind from my sails, though in all honesty I didn't think she felt at all confrontational.

"There has been a mistake," I insisted. "Up to three are to be taken over a twenty four hour period as and when she needs them. I explained this very clearly on the printed sheet I gave to Mr. Brown on the day Minty moved in. I understood everyone would be given a copy. Is that not so?"

I felt the weakness now of being one against two who, having followed a written instruction from the chemist, had right on their side. Mrs. Quin was quick to capitalise, and evaded my question. "That's why we needed to have direct access to the prescriptions - better if we collect from our chemist here in town now that Minty is in our care."

Why did I feel she was thinking they had come to the rescue of someone who had not been cared for adequately for over forty years, and in doing so had also to cope with a degenerating mother who was incapable of dealing with such complicated things as prescriptions?

"Look at the packets issued previously - you will see the correct instruction there," I persisted. But of course those packets had been destroyed. I was limp with the worry of the preceding day. "I can see how the error occurred," I conceded, "but it doesn't excuse giving them in the morning. They were soporific and caused a great deal of distress." Again I referred to the call I had had from the Centre and stressed my daughter's fear she had been overdosed.

Whilst assuring me she had not given them in the morning, her smile registered neither guilt nor offence at being wrongly blamed. But neither, to me, did she appear concerned that someone for whom she was in 'loco parentis,' had been so distraught.

Surely Minty hadn't got it wrong. She had said they were given when she woke up. She was so meticulous about her pills; always had been. In fact wouldn't go anywhere without her three clobazam that made such a significant difference to her day. And never, ever, had she taken three at once. It was inconceivable to me that she would have been so frightened by being given pills in the morning if that hadn't been the case, yet I was aware of the futility of continuing down this path without proof. It would be her word against the carer's. And who would believe the one against the other?

"Perhaps you'll allow me to phone our surgery from your office?" I asked. "I wish to clarify the instruction from the consultant in your hearing. Then at least Minty can be allowed to have the tablets at the time of need."

"Of course. But then we'll need to have it in writing from the consultant. And I'm afraid it won't be possible to break in halves the pills that are prescribed for alternate days. They must be administered exactly as per the pharmacy instruction."

Correctly, but for me infuriatingly, she was going by the book, and meanwhile my heart was pounding as I enacted calm and tried to quell the agitation that surged.

Our surgery confirmed what I had written down on that first day, which must have corresponded with the instructions on the packets at that time. I withdrew to write a note to the consultant asking him to re-state that the pills were to be taken as and when needed, thereby necessitating self-medication. Once done I returned to the office to realise the tension was all on my side for they were already in relaxed conversation.

"Perhaps we can address the administration of the medication now?" I asked, and repeated the agreement I had reached prior to Minty's entry.

The Deputy explained very amiably that she wasn't happy with packets of pills in Minty's room, as if I were making the request for the first time. It was not the safest situation for other residents for whom she also had responsibility.

"But that's why you were going to install a lockable box or cabinet," I said turning from one to the other.

"It's on order," Mr. Brown replied casting the briefest glance at his Deputy as if ascertaining that were the case.

The bed, the carpet, the box - all 'in hand' But they should have already been there, awaiting her arrival. And residents didn't go into each other's rooms unless invited.

"But of course they might." I was told.

"And without the packets she can't read the tiny print on the backing foil," I said. "I explained about her poor eyesight - in fact I stressed the effects of it in the notes you specifically asked for. Surely they were communicated?"

"I know what I can get for her," Mrs. Quin said with the spontaneous kindness of a sudden idea. And my question was left hanging on the air. "A seven day box with a compartment for each day. Then Minty can have her week's supply and I'll have the bulk locked in the in office medicine cupboard."

Mr. Brown smiled broadly as if all was now resolved by this inspired compromise, and with everyone happy they could get on with whatever my arrival had interrupted. But why hadn't this discussion taken place months before, instead of the autonomous replies to all my questions. It was obvious now that further than the concession she had just offered, the Deputy was unable to go. Doubtless she was acting professionally according to policy and within the law, and gave me the impression it would only be a matter of time before I realised this.

For my part I had encountered on many occasions, a similar untroubled attitude in people often adored by Minty. And while she lived at home it was of no consequence because I was there to fill the gaps, oil the wheels and generally be the button that held things together. She could enjoy those with no sensitive sense of urgency, or ones slower to pick up on angst and atmosphere because at the end of the day she wasn't totally dependent on them.

I was drained, but knew that whether or not it had been considered 'a storm in a teacup,' I must stand my ground and make them aware of the effect the incident had had. Minty had been frightened enough to think she might die, and if the Deputy were to regain her trust then bridges would have to be built. It would be to everyone's benefit if Mrs. Quin would visit Minty in her room, sit with her and explain how the 'mistake' had happened.

Without it, whether or not she thought it had been trivial, she would lose Minty's trust for always, and not without repercussions. I knew my daughter too well to believe it could be any different. Lack of intellect she may have, but intuition and memory she has in abundance. She has many times left me speechless by her recall, and when something has had a profound effect, whether good or ill, it is indelibly, and indefinitely, etched on her mind.

It was essential that the effect of this particular situation be erased before it could take a destructive hold. I repeated my request that she should please understand how important it was to get my daughter back on side. An apology, if only for having unintentionally caused her to be frightened, would meet with instant 'forgiveness' for Minty hated disharmony. At no time did I feel she had grasped the significance of the error's impact on the person who had been so badly affected.

Yes, her reaction may have been coloured by the soaps she watches; might even been seen as amusing when the dust had settled. It was surely a question of perception. If it's inside your head that you have been overdosed, it's as real as if it happened. And I needed the Deputy to understand that.

But you can signal and signal and sometimes the relevant people take no notice. I could tell that from her point of view there wasn't a justified complaint in so far as the error hadn't been hers, and that my irrational reaction must be excused because I was worrying pointlessly about a problem that really didn't exist.

Meanwhile a pillbox with the days of the week printed on each section, would be purchased. It was a compromise to Minty's capability, and to safeguard everyone's interest. With this done, though I could not concur, it was felt that any agreement I had reached with Mr. Brown was being honoured. It was also her intention to request a change of wrapping on the pills, and it would help if I could let them have some of the most recent prescription until the change could be effected.

"And we are sorry about her not going to her job today," Mr. Brown said. "Duty staff will now phone either of us if no one is available to take her, and Mrs. Quin will come in specially to do the drive."

"It will be no problem at all," the Deputy smiled. "I shall be happy to do it."

Though I felt the offer to be sincere, again it was immediacy rather than forethought. Surely she couldn't believe that covering for the drive was more important than building a bridge re the pills? I felt she still wasn't convinced she had lost Minty's trust, or that action needed to be taken to regain it; a stance to which rightly or wrongly, I could only attribute a surprising lack of sensitivity.

I made a further attempt. "I'm grateful for your offer, but am begging you to talk with her about the pills. It is terribly important to her wanting to be here."

"Of course," it was smilingly agreed.

In an effort to move my daughter beyond the situation, I suggested she invited me for coffee. We took a tray and sat on the couch and I asked her if she would like to put some of her photographs in the sitting room she shared with the other people in her block but she insisted it was Peter's sitting room. It wasn't difficult to see why - his family photographs were on the wall, his box of sweets and magazines on the coffee table and his shoes and slippers under the couch.

I wondered why it seemed singularly his, and no-one else's, and learned that the others enjoyed their music more, or didn't like television so rarely sat in the lounge. Peter liked some of the soaps Minty enjoyed, but he also loved sport, and when that was on she was welcome to watch it with him or use the television in her own room.

Assuming he hadn't got a personal television I asked tentatively of staff whether they could encourage Minty to put just one or two personal items in the lounge so that she could feel she had a stake in it, even if she continued to watch TV in her bedroom.

"But he has - they all have!" Hugh said. "We'll tell him he has to share the lounge TV and to take turns going to watch in his room occasionally."

Later in the year, the diary provided enlightenment
I liked watching the soaps with Peter. We know each other a long time and are friends. When he want to watch he tell me go in my room because the sitting room is his. He has own armchair and table

with his choc on, and his shoes under his seat – lots of them so he can choose ones to wear every day. He keeps them there and not in his bedroom. A staff told him to share the TV but he didn't because it was his home. So I went to my room and watch Holby City. I like my room when I come. Now it feels lonely, not like my room at home and I missed mum coming in with coffee together. I love my home but mum and I doing this so I have another home. Lots of times I shook. Every night after Coronation St I go my room because Peter wants to watch Millionaire. It is his tele because he here for long time. I miss my mum's goodnight cuddle and our plans for next day. I like our plannings and doing lots of nice things.

There were dark rings under her eyes and I knew she hadn't slept well after the pill episode.

"Why don't you have a nap whilst I prepare supper," I said when we got home. "We'll have it by the fire and then watch a film together if you'd like to."

I was thankful I had reined in the anger I had felt earlier, and when later I hugged her goodnight I told her that perhaps after all the mistake hadn't been quite as bad as we had thought, especially as the three pills were given at night.

She said quietly, but with absolute conviction, "It was morning time. I went for my breakfast and when I came back to my room to get ready for Centre, Mrs. Quin sat on my bed and she said here are your tablets and I told her I didn't take them all at once but she say I must."

I asked her if at any time the words had been spoken harshly or crossly. But no, Mrs. Quin had 'said very kindly words.' And I tried to imagine the conversation. Perhaps she was asked if she had taken three herself, and when she would have said 'no,' it might have been thought – given the new instruction on the packet - that the night duty carer had forgotten, hence why the dosage was hastily 'rectified' in the morning.

Now I was worried. If human error had occurred, and one must accept that it can and does, and if Minty was right, then during our meeting, had accuracy and truth been evaded? It didn't make for an easy mind. Absolutely no sign of any vindictiveness; quite the opposite in fact, but I must be vigilant.

I had not then seen the diary in which Minty had written:
Mrs.Q bring me pills 3 at once and say I must. At centre I phoned mum and told her. She know what to do. I scared. I don't want to stay here.
When I got back I watched Neighbours with Peter, and Grace call us for tea and at night I had thumping head. I was shaking and hadn't got the clobazam I needed. All night I shooked and wanted Mum. Safe at home. Grace say in morning 'You look ever so white. Do you feel ok. I was just tired and couldn't go to the Centre.

Having driven Minty back for Sunday lunch, I deposited a note into the office indicating I had put fifteen of the pills I was keeping for weekends, in her drawer, i.e. for up to three per day that had been requested until they could change the bubble wrapped for individually sealed ones, and hoped this would help them. By acceding to Mrs. Quin's request I hoped in turn to elicit her cooperation so that we could work as a team in my daughter's interests.

Determined there should be no repetition of the occurrence, I sent copies of my correspondence re the pills to our Social Worker, and making my concern crystal clear, emphasised the importance of regaining trust. Diplomacy is about knowing when to bend and when to stand firm, and on this one I refused to compromise.

I have no idea whether she picked up on the concern, for I received no reaction in any form.

CHAPTER ELEVEN

On Monday evening such a bubbling voice responded to my call. She had not gone to the Centre because apparently it was the day arranged for her 'one-to-one' with her special carer. Had it been planned for some time or was it a result of my concern of the previous days? And if not for the latter reason, would it not have been better to plan it for the one day of the week she took off from the Centre? No matter. They had gone to lunch together and then to the latest Harry Potter film and she couldn't wait for another such super day.

She had always related to those in charge of her routine rather than her peers and if she was developing a good relationship with the young carer who obviously meant a lot to her, then the unease she felt about Emily would be less important, and maybe after all, everything would be resolved.

Next evening however, she was subdued. That something was amiss was obvious. During the course of the conversation it became clear that Mrs. Quin was on duty and thus there was an obvious fear of a repeat of the pill ordeal. When Minty rang off and went to watch TV, I telephoned Mrs. Quin to repeat my request that she build bridges and explain that it had all been a misunderstanding. I was putting words into her mouth but with no power to make her swallow them.

She was delightfully pleasant and reassuring and said that of course she would, but to my knowledge - and Minty would certainly have mentioned it - no such conversation ever took place. The next time she was home for the weekend I asked if she now felt more comfortable with Mrs. Quin, but it seemed to me there had been no attempt to bond. If that was so, it was a discarded opportunity that was to prove instrumental in the final decision.

* * *

I felt so gutted when she wasn't excited, yet not all days at home had been exciting. 'Let me know what to do,' I pleaded to the silence that now replaced her. I mustn't step backwards but see it through as if she had gone away on a long holiday. But she hadn't. Nor to university where enduring the rigours and missing home was all part of achieving her goals. We had a quite different objective: we were trying to find where she would be happy for the rest of her life in the event of my predeceasing her.

I felt no urge to get up next morning - how much Minty was my purpose. Somehow the day was got through and when I phoned in the evening she seemed brighter again. She had had a good day and better still they were going to have a meeting with Mr. Brown to discuss the lounge and how it belonged to everyone. I was grateful to him for she needed to feel this was her second home.

And I think the meeting was productive in that they elicited Peter's voiced cooperation. I'm sure staff meant to continue but with the other residents making greater demands on their time, and Mr. Brown only in for half the week, Peter was able to resist the pressure and the lounge remained essentially 'his'.

Meanwhile the days dragged as if the world were struggling to engage first gear. Days when she was hesitant, unsure, and, to me, unconvincingly happy. Sometimes tiny stress lines played around her mouth - always a give-away that told me that all was not yet totally right. It is impossible to live with someone for so long without developing an awareness of the sentiment behind the sudden hitch to the shoulder or flicker in the eye. On some days she was much brighter; different entirely. A pattern hadn't evolved yet.

Gradually it became evident that our evening conversations on the 'happy' days seemed to end with, 'So and so is on duty - I like them. They're fun.' It was plain that staff affected her outlook significantly more than anything else and I began to keep a record.

And although still finding Emily overbearing and noisy, she was somewhat better able to cope when favourite staff members were available to help. What continued to concern me greatly was the dreadful tiredness; a state that couldn't be allowed to continue indefinitely.

Invariably Saturdays passed at the speed of light. On one of them early in January I had planned for us to go to an inn not far from home and where we could sit by an enormous fire, but by lunchtime Minty had settled for staying by our own fire with a huge mug of coffee.

"Home's nice," she said. And I realised that living between the two could be tiring and that she wouldn't want to go out for a change of scene in the way that she might when spending every day at the same address. I wasn't prepared for her next question, and as so often is the case, realised just how deep her thinking often is.

"When will the other girls come?"

"Which other girls?"

"Anna and Jenny we met at Home Farm. You remember." There was earnestness in her voice now.

I delved into recollections of conversations we had had over the past weeks and at no time had they been a part of them.

"I expect they're still there. We haven't been in touch for awhile have we?"

"But if the man said it wasn't possible for me to go there, then they'll be looking for somewhere to live too."

When Lord Rix listed the expected virtues of those who sat in the House of Lords, he asserted there are people with a learning disability who also fit the job-description admirably. He had included 'common sense' and 'an instinct for justice.' I wished he could have been with us now for he would have applauded her approach, and felt for me as I sought to explain the inequities of 'the system.'

We walked down the lane in the wintry sunshine before she went for her nap. Only with her asleep could I bring myself to do jobs that took me away from her presence. Every second counted and I would miss none of them, and yet I knew she wanted to come home for weekends without my fussing over her every moment.

Finally the Sunday came when it wasn't so hard and I left her without tears biting the back of my eyes. As soon as she saw Greg Sarah and Jane on duty, she relaxed. And I knew that though still an essential, the time had come to accept I was no longer the *only* factor and support in her life.

"Phone me tonight mum," she said. She was still in transition, but more confident. But I could not let go of the plea 'Please God let me outlive her.' Would this be enough if it were *all* she had; if I couldn't come and take her shopping and out to lunch on Thursdays and for treats at weekends? Whilst I had yet to be convinced, I still hoped for it to happen. 'It was,' a well meaning friend insisted, 'a mistake to find somewhere so close to home where I could see all the teething troubles. And wasn't it enough that she was warm, well fed, and cared for?' And the simple, unequivocal answer to her question was that it most certainly was not.

Next Thursday we went to town for some new shoes for her and I wondered how she would manage to buy them out of the 'less than seventeen pounds' if no one was helping her to save a little each week. As we looked along the rows and she chose a pair she liked, an assistant approached and asked her what size she needed. Minty looked at her earnestly, somewhat bemused by the question.

"A size to fit my feet," she replied, obviously wondering why a simple situation should be made so complicated! I surreptitiously indicated size two and a very satisfied customer left the shop.

"What did you have for supper last night?" she asked suddenly, and it wasn't a good idea to admit that without her I hadn't bothered. Logically I should have had more time with Minty away, but the visiting, writing messages for staff, phoning, and generally worrying myself into a pathetic muddle, left precious few hours to organise life at base. Life was harder when she was away, for my mind never left her.

"Pork chop with mushrooms," I lied, and asked what she had had.

"Jacket potato," she said. "I like mushrooms."

"Again?" And then not to give her a hint of concern added, "You mean you had jacket potato and mushrooms?"

"No. Jacket potato."

"Did everyone have jacket potato?"

She shook her head. "Shepherd's pie and baked beans. Charley's a very clever cook"

I squirmed involuntarily at the combination, then determined to maintain an unworried stance, grinned. "Couldn't you have had shepherd's pie too?"

"It was fattening with lots of butter, and I know jacket potato isn't. So when Charley asked me what I like to have, I said that. And I go and make a sandwich later on if I'm hungry!"

"But you could have asked Charley not to put butter in your mashed potato," I offered, thinking it would have been no problem to make a separate dish given that each was to have according to need. That way she would at least have had some protein. I must resume the veggie battle.

"He couldn't take the butter out when he opened the packet Mum! Silly old you!"

The pattern was emerging. She had had no meat or fish other than at the weekend, for a week now; in fact a jacket potato every evening. And I could guess how it was happening. I had involved her in meal planning at home for years to help her understand how she could avoid the obesity so often associated with Downs. Each evening she was most likely being offered whatever had been bought, and she, recognising the calorific potential of the chosen meal, and to avoid causing inconvenience or being a bother, would offer to have a jacket potato.

I hadn't the slightest doubt, given the nature of her carers that she would have been asked what they could do for her if she didn't 'like' the menu. And because each evening there was a different carer on duty, they would not have known that in order to be no trouble and unable to tell them how to reduce the calories in the purchased meals (which she would actually have loved and was trying to resist), she had suggested the same alternative to each of their colleagues. They were much the same age as my own sons and I couldn't imagine *them* peeling vast amounts of vegetables or cooking from scratch.

Had there been a resident cook, she would have been aware of the repetition and indeed any dietary omissions. And if they had elected to dispense with a cook because this gave an extra salary to enable the purchase of the best carers, then someone ought to be keeping a record and monitoring a weekly menu chart.

I had intended to take her back immediately after buying the shoes so as to maximise on the familiarity that was now growing. Instead I tweaked her nose and said, "Come on, I'll treat you for lunch." I knew exactly the right place, renowned for its healthy home cooking.

"That was nice," she enthused after putting away a tender chicken breast and a variety of green vegetables. "You and I have fun together don't we?" She had eaten with relish but was tired now.

On return I told Grace of my concern. She would be on duty tonight and I was right in my supposition that she, and presumably other carers, didn't know that Minty had had so many jacket potatoes. But *someone* ought to have known. When I phoned that evening she had fish and fresh vegetables that Grace had cooked!

But what about tomorrow, and the day after? And who would have taken her for lunch had I been dead? And just how many jacket potatoes and late night sandwiches with the resulting weight gain, would there have been if I hadn't been around to intervene?

It wasn't the first time Minty's compliance and reluctance to cause anyone any bother had been a problem. It was always a battle to get her to declare what she wanted, what she liked, or where she wanted to go. For in truth, much more important to her was *who* she was to go or do something *with*. As for what she wanted, that was easy - harmony, with everyone happy. Whatever achieved that end was what she wanted to do.

And I had, after all, committed this to paper. The Manager had read it and pronounced it helpful. Now I wondered if it had merited notice when he passed it on. Or had it just been filed away?

* * *

She was soon to spend a day in hospital for investigative purposes and though I had written to this effect I had received no

110

response. Perhaps it was assumed I would take their cooperation as read. I had to know they were aware of the necessary preparation and phoned to speak with the Deputy. She wouldn't however be on duty until next day and 'would no doubt call me.'

Though I had woken long before dawn I resisted the urge to close my eyes that afternoon in case I missed her call, but none came and thinking the message hadn't been passed on I rang several times before making contact. It was essential that on the days preceding her admission Minty adhered to the strict dietary regime I had indicated.

There would be no problem at all, I was informed most affably, and yes my message had been received. I wasn't to worry. But if she didn't want me to worry, why not phone at least to acknowledge my request? Was I being petty? Too demanding? I didn't know *who* I was these days let alone *what* I was.

Meanwhile the Social Worker phoned though didn't allude to the copy correspondence I had sent following the pill episode. I registered my concern that bridges hadn't been built and too that the companionship might not be sufficient if I were not around. She said merely that there would be soon be a review when my opinions could be given an airing and meanwhile it would be a good idea to make plans of my own. I refrained from saying that plans were something I would be able to make once my mind was clear of more important considerations.

* * *

Minty's trust in the medical profession is absolute and she watched carefully as all the preliminary procedures were dealt with. She nonetheless provoked a smile or two when, knee deep in her 'Health and Safety' course at the local college, she asked a senior consultant if he had remembered to wash his hands.

It was a rough time for her, but once it was over she brightened and though I yearned to bring her home she was becoming accustomed to being away and I must do nothing to impede the progress. I saw her into bed, stayed until her eyelids closed and then handed over the diet sheet from the hospital, which stressed she must have fresh vegetables on the days following. It

111

was essential. I asked that they keep the closest eye on her and apologised in advance that I would be phoning often that evening until I knew she was sleeping soundly.

I thought she would have woken after her nap with a healthy hunger and was distressed to be told she had had an uncomfortable time for an hour or so but was recuperating now.

"I'll come over," I said as if responding to a call from the hospital, but it was insisted all was well and I knew that if this was to work I mustn't cling, but stay in the background trusting them to care for her. Sarah, angel that she was, would steam some light fish for her tea.

To my relief the staff members on duty were all ones Minty liked and they promised to check on her frequently and call if there was any cause for concern. She had had some pain but each hour had brought an improvement.

"She won't trouble you," I told Hugh. She'll say she's all right rather than be a bother. So may I please phone you every hour - and on the office phone so that I don't wake her by calling on the one outside her door?"

I apologised for being what they must now think was a nightmare of a mother. And wonderful character that he was, he said only, "You're a bit like the one I've got. Call as often as you like."

The longing to be with her was fierce but opposed to this powerful urge was the will to help her settle. Impotent now to help or comfort her, I could only wonder what madness we had embarked on. But we *had*, and the least I could do for her was to help make it work.

It was Friday and I would normally have collected Minty from her nursery job but she hadn't felt up to going, and because she had had a day at home prior to hospital, we would do the sensible thing and wait until Saturday to begin the weekend. Mr. Brown was there when I arrived and in the few minutes we were able to speak before he was called to the phone he told me that Charley had gained promotion and would be leaving very soon. That was a real blow. Charley had so much potential, a genuine rapport with his charges,

112

and would be considerable loss. If only he could stay just a few more months.

Minty seemed fully recovered and we spent a couple of hours in town before coming home. Though pleased with her purchases she was soon tired and slept for the afternoon before laying the table for our special weekly candlelit supper. Instinct told me this was not just a normal tiredness following her hospital stay, but more fundamental and I observed carefully until, as always, the hours sped and it was Sunday again. She had put on weight despite eating so little in the last few days, recognised it herself, and elected not to return for the substantial Sunday lunch.

"You cook," she said. "Then I won't get fat. I'll go back for tea."

A young woman I hadn't met though Minty obviously knew her, greeted her warmly. Drawing her into the kitchen, she took her hand and my heart sank as she trilled, "Look, I've got your favourite jacket potato - and I've done some spaghetti to go with it!"
Minty glanced in my direction and we both grinned. "Eat a tiny bit of it," I whispered, knowing she wouldn't hurt the carer's feelings for the world. "I've put some fruit-salady stuff in your room. I'll go and have another word in the office."
Grace was on duty and I was preaching to the converted.

"I will raise it," she promised.

"And I'll leave yet another note," I said. "She has had fresh veg at home today and it's imperative she continues, especially over the coming days." I wanted to say 'always' but the first objective must be to clear the immediate hurdle.
Grace looked for the hospital sheet I had provided and meanwhile I discreetly scanned the notice board.

"I've brought another copy," I said, and deduced from her expression it was the first time she had seen it.

Minty's diary entry after her hospital visit, months later revealed the following:-
Emily's turn to wash up but she wouldn't so I couldn't dry. Sarah said You not well and she took me for a bath and made me fresh. She is kind. I missed mum. I had awful thumping head and Sarah took me to my room and I had spasm all night. Emily play her music and I

113

still can't sleep and morning comes. Grace asked her calm down a bit and she wouldn't and she made Grace stressed out. I don't like it when people upset but Grace say she not cross with me only Emily. She gave me a cuddle and clobazam because I shook all night.

A different night Greg went in to Emily. I heard him tell Emily I trying to sleep and be quiet and Emily came out and banged her door and Grace told her off. Emily shout I don't like Minty. I want to go home and not live with Emily.

On the dreary way home I allowed the release of tears. It was pointless my talking to individual members of staff: it had to come from the top at a staff meeting. Most certainly I would raise it at the review when I could finally pressure Social Services into having it. According to the paperwork it should already have taken place. Now it was urgent. Again, the question nagged. 'What if I were not here? Who would be fighting her corner?'

After three fruitless hours of trying to track down the relevant personnel at Social Services, I phoned Greenlands. Fortuitously Mrs. Quin took my call and I asked if the bubble wrapped pills had yet been exchanged for her to repay the ones I had loaned. Then, implying an assumption that efficiency between various agencies must have decreed that a date had now been fixed for the review, I asked her to confirm it. She would phone me next day.

By evening I hadn't heard from her and decided to be a nuisance after the customary chat with Minty who was brighter tonight. But Mrs. Quin was out. It was eight when we made contact, and I repeated my questions, starting with the pills. It seemed it had been decided to wait until the next batch order was given to the chemist, and thus it wouldn't be possible to repay the ones lent. And after all they were now in charge of medication and Minty would be given whatever number was due for days out with me, which really made 'repayment' irrelevant.

Uncharitably 'Not got around to it?' went through my mind. What if she was ill and couldn't return as expected, or if she left for the Day Nursery and forgot to take them with her? Surely it was sensible to have a standby reserve at both ends?

"But Greenlands was her base now. Someone would bring them out to her wherever she was." The voice was gentle but the words went home like an arrow. Was I being uncooperative, or not meeting them half way by remaining unconvinced? And surely if something that had been agreed was to be revoked, it would have been courteous to phone me rather than wait for me to call and find out?

I explained again that her prescription couldn't be neatly synchronised because whilst the dosage of two of her medications remained constant, two could vary according to need. That was of no consequence; the full supply would be ordered on a regular monthly basis and surplus pills destroyed as the law required. I was horrified. There were notices in every surgery advising how much money was being wasted by careless use of the health services, missed appointments and wasted pills.

Having lived with bureaucracy and 'legal requirements' for so long, such a proposed wastage, although shocking, did not surprise me. I decided to waste no further energy on the matter and move to another priority, that of the 'review.' Still no date had yet been arranged though it would 'probably be soon.' I didn't want to cause antipathy that might impact on my daughter by speaking as frankly as I wished and instead put another call through to Social Services next morning and faxed a further reminder about diet before driving to the surgery.

Our GP had become a friend over the years and I told him that Greenlands wished to transfer Minty to a doctor closer to them 'for the obvious sensible reasons,' but that as long as I was able to drive I was in no haste to change. In fact until other aspects were in a less tenuous state, I would resist the request.

"We won't rush to be sensible," he smiled. "We'll keep things as they are until we know it's permanent. But they're right. It would be difficult for me to visit her from this distance nor would she be brought to my surgery if you weren't here."

"But I am. I know one day I won't be but...."

"Exactly. So for now you bring her to me as you've always done."

* * *

Long before the offer of a place at Greenlands was offered, we had agreed to go away with friends for a long weekend. Greg had given her a supply of pills to cover the days away and said he hoped we'd have a super time. I noticed he said 'we' which I appreciated. I hadn't felt like part of a 'we' on my last visit.

Noticing immediately the white face, I suggested supper and an early bedtime pretending it was for our joint benefit to enable us to be fresh for the long drive. She took her evening dose from the package and I realised there were three pills short. Greg hadn't yet gone off duty when I phoned and having prepared the medication himself, he was perplexed. It soon became clear why we differed on the number she should have.

"It's policy to count the pills residents have at four o'clock each day, and then deduct that number from the supply needed for the following twenty four hours," he told me.

"But it's between tea time and late evening that she most needs them," I explained, "and because I gave all my supply to Mrs. Quin I don't have any in the house…"

He was obviously concerned and I knew that as senior person on duty he would not have wished to put me in a difficult position.

"Will you still be there if I drive to you now? It will take about half an hour," I asked.

"Yes, and I'm really sorry about this. I know you're preparing to go away, but I can't leave base to come to you."

So out came the car again. Another drive through the traffic.

Frustration rose to the surface. So it was policy that the arbitrary time of 4pm had been established. Well, policy it may be, but I felt darned sure it wasn't law. Or if so the law was the proverbial ass.

He was apologetic that I'd had to return though he had made no error according to the rules. We discussed the situation and I asked if, until I could raise it at the review, he would challenge the choice of timing at the next staff meeting. He would try, he agreed, and his choice of phrase made me wonder if he needed to try to raise it, or try to get it changed. The thought of voicing yet another issue filled me with apprehension in case none would be taken seriously. But I hadn't raised 'lots' of issues - only the same ones lots of times.

Minty was already asleep when I got back. We wouldn't be leaving early, I decided. We'd go when she was thoroughly rested. And as soon as we returned I'd tell our GP about the pill shortage situation.

* * *

"Bureaucracy," he sighed, raising his hands in a despairing gesture, and promptly writing out a prescription. "Keep these at home and have peace of mind."

He kept his hand over the prescription for a while and then said, "Sure all this is worth it?"

"I don't know yet," I replied. "But until I do, all you have to do is to keep me alive."

"Well you look, and therefore I assume you feel, ten years older than two months ago. And you know I don't have any magic to make you young again."

"I'm not asking you to make me younger," I said weakly. "Just make sure I get older - hundred and two if you can."

"That'll be a joint effort. And you might be the one putting it at risk right now."

"I have to try a bit longer. Maybe it'll come right."

"But not by putting yourself into an early grave." He looked over the top of his glasses philosophically. "You know people like your girl are often more susceptible to infection than the rest of us."

He said it almost apologetically and the gentleness with which he spoke served only to increase the doubt in me. If there was any likelihood at all of her pre-deceasing me, I didn't have to find an alternative home.

Oh for a glimpse into the future. Though I recognised the futility of such a wish, at least I'd have a better idea of what to do, how to plan and which path to take.

I recalled as a child, long hours of discussion with my grandmother. She loved words too much to waste them on inconsequential detail and I found in her a soul mate with whom to discuss the things that interested me. Whilst I no longer remember the detail of conversations or the reason for them taking place, one of her replies will forever stay with me. Someone we both knew had died and there followed from me the 'why, when she wasn't old had she been ill and why hadn't she been in bed, and would her parents be sad' etc.

I listened intently to her, for those times were the pearls of my young life, and must then have asked when she herself would die, fearing the answer now that I knew people much younger could suddenly expire. She didn't pause, or weigh her words, but said simply, "I shall die when I've stopped being any use to anyone; when no one needs me any more."

Illogical, irrational, erroneous even, that response was lodged in my young mind and has resolutely remained cemented there ever since; has indeed been a solace ever since I have cared for my 'Peter Pan.' Words that have whispered comfort whilst fears of predeceasing her have raged in my head; a concept that is often submerged by more rational anxiety, but floats again to the surface to calm me when it is less frightening to trust my Gran's philosophy than my own logic.

CHAPTER TWELVE

Dismayed, I discovered that the request for fresh vegetables seemed largely to have gone unheeded. I didn't feel it was because staff members were young, rather that they were unaware of the importance of the situation, which at this point in time was a medical one. It could all have been so simple, and was instead so unnecessarily wearing as I visited to plug the gaps.

My spirits rose however when Minty was so cheerful during an evening phone call, the reason soon becoming evident. She had been to the hairdresser for the second time in less than two weeks and wanted me to see the result. In the normal circumstances of living at home this was of no concern. She used her allowance for whatever she needed or wanted. But she had had to withdraw twenty pounds from the amount I had deposited for her daily expenses, whilst I continued to take in everyday toiletries and hobby materials.

If she tried to purchase those, then hairdressing, apart from the monthly trim, would hardly be an option. Who was helping her to budget? And what happened when she needed clothes and shoes when I wasn't around? Tactful, roundabout enquiries revealed that if she wanted to do something and hadn't withdrawn the weekly amount specified as being left after paying rent etc, via the office, there was no objection. Later events revealed that I would have been wiser to have asked her to withdraw money for personal needs, but lack of simple communication had left me unaware of the workings of the system.

"Come and see it now because it won't last until morning!" she said excitedly, and I could only think that a hairdo would have been fine if it had coincided with an evening out.

Her usual short, natural style had been converted into the latest spiky fashion with more than a little help from quantities of mousse and lacquer. She ate the coleslaw I had taken for her, and then as we sipped coffee, her eyes began to close.

"I think you'll have to put that new hairstyle to bed," I whispered, but her head was already on the pillow. I moulded the bedclothes around her and kissed her gently. She would be so disappointed when she woke, and the fashion statement was no more.

* * *

Battle was resumed as I rang Social Services to ask again for the review. I needed to voice my concerns and for them to be recorded. It would also provide an opportunity to ask about budgeting, and for them to tell me how my own perceptions might be wrong.

It wasn't a good move. The Social Worker clearly enunciated 'policy' several times, and if things were being done according to 'policy' then I had no grounds for requesting otherwise. Clearly the subject had been raised and medication discussed, and she had been persuaded that action taken had been reasonable. But she *hadn't* been present at the discussions I had had prior to Minty's entry.

And it's so easy to tell someone 'it's the rule'. No need to think any more or find a better way. It can be set in stone until another government directive ripples the pond. I had the very strong impression I'd succeeded in putting them all on the same side of the fence. And that wasn't on my side. I'd made so many wrong decisions in my life, and this was one I *had* to get right.

The typed policy stating aims and objectives had indicated that 'medication would be administered in a manner respectful to residents', but also that 'wherever possible residents would have the opportunity to self-administer.' I had taken Mr. Brown's word; had accepted his assurance that her independence would be preserved and indeed encouraged. I hadn't felt that my interpretation of our agreement differed from his, but it was clearly at odds with interpretation on site.

I put it to the Social Worker that the review would do no less than provide an opportunity to enable better understanding between us. She still wasn't sure when the meeting could take place for they were 'snowed under' and dealing with so many more urgent matters. She would try to attend to it tomorrow but 'couldn't promise.' But I was less accepting of such statements than I had been in the days when she told me it would be unreasonable to expect Minty to receive attention whilst I was standing and breathing, only for this to go out of the window weeks later, and I stood my ground. It was after all, also *policy* to have had a review meeting before now for the very purpose of discussing concerns on either side, and presumably to aid the client to settle.

Within half an hour, she had rung back. Despite being snowed under, suddenly a review would take place two weeks to the day. With hindsight I suppose I was seeking support, another viewpoint or criticism even. Any communication at all to help me clear the muddle that was crowding my brain, but it was obvious that grappling with a hot potato was the last thing she wanted to do before the review.

It was a Thursday again and I called to take Minty out for an hour or so over the lunch hour. Mr. Brown was on the defensive as soon as I arrived, and it wasn't difficult to guess that he had had a call from the Social Worker alerting him of our conversation. Hence the hastily arranged meeting. He was uncomfortable; I much less so now that I had a firm date, and felt no awkwardness in conversing. He told me that my fax of yesterday had 'come through all black' and the Deputy had been unable to read anything other than my name and fax number on the top of the page. So why not phone to say it was illegible? I was mystified.

I could only draw the conclusion that I was either of no importance; totally irrelevant to her, or that I had in some way caused her to have no wish to communicate with me. Perhaps she saw relatives as an unnecessary encumbrance and only the residents had significance. And I could have lived with that, been happy to be insignificant if only bridges had been built after losing Minty's trust over the pill episode, and importance attached to her dietary requirements.

I decided the only way to ease the tension was to say that I was grateful that a meeting had been arranged when I was sure we would be able to iron out some of the difficulties, though I didn't feel that the Deputy thought there were any. Mr. Brown replied only that he wouldn't ask her to do anything 'contrary to policy.' Again the word that propped up stances in potential confrontational situations. But who wanted confrontation? Certainly not I. I was bewildered by what I sensed to be unvoiced antagonism.

It was as if our meetings in the summer had never occurred. I wouldn't dream of asking for policy to be contravened had the policy been the one agreed, i.e. that she could self-administer from a medicine cabinet in her room - a cabinet, I reminded him as tactfully as I could, that had yet to materialise. Had all who worked for Joe Public become so 'litigation aware' that they now saw trouble where none existed? It certainly seemed so.

* * *

I wasn't surprised when I phoned Minty in the evening to learn she had not had jacket potato, but a fish parcel in sauce, albeit from a packet – and with fresh vegetables. The 'real' cooking was obviously reserved for weekends, and now she was reluctant to return for it because it had still not been possible to substitute the roast potatoes for less calorie laden boiled ones.

Excellent fare worthy of a top restaurant and that she loved, but she wanted even more to avoid becoming gross. And the irony was that she had already gained her hard-lost weight during her own unaided attempt not to do so. The promise that 'each would eat according to need' would have required so little effort just by avoiding a heavy intake of fat. Any dietician worth her salt could have made it work and without all these apparently irritating reminders from mother.

I felt impotent, ineffective, and excluded.

Deciding the best course of action was to concentrate on something else for an hour or so that evening, I sat in front of the screen, but no words would come. I made a sandwich and forgot to eat it; pondered various jobs that needed attention, and accomplished virtually nothing.   Beaten and drained I wondered why was everything such a battle and why it was such an unreasonable expectation to be involved in the greatest change to my modus vivendi in over forty years. Was it a lack of trust? Mr. Brown hadn't given that impression; had in fact several times admitted how hard he would find the situation if he had to hand over the care of his own children.

Why could I not rid myself of the feeling they were acting on the premise I was already dead? There was an informed awareness of legal obligations, but an apparent corresponding lack of sensitivity to the meaningful details involved in the relationship between carer and cared-for. *They* were now caring for my daughter and must cover themselves in law. Of course I understood that.

The only rational conclusion I could draw was that whilst Mr. Brown had genuinely seemed to think we were in tandem, the person in daily charge, and who should have been present at our meetings, had built up no such rapport with me. I recalled the evening Minty had gone for a Christmas meal prior to moving in, Mrs. Quin hadn't joined in the general introductions; had in fact made no overture to me at all.

She didn't know me in the least at that point, so I must assume it had been a case of instant dislike. Had I spent the time with her that her seniority merited, or been aware that I had mistaken identities on the festive evening, I would have been cautious, recognising that however kind a person she was, she would not evoke the confidence to enable my daughter to settle happily. Minty has too many of my genes for that to have been possible.

When I collected Minty from the Day Nursery to bring her home for the weekend her eyes were tired and red; she herself pale, listless. She nodded off before we reached home, and was in bed and asleep half an hour later. When she woke she was very tearful, not with misery, but seemingly sleep deprivation.   A light sleeper, her companion's loud music, tendency to bang doors and shout was continuing to affect her adversely. And still uppermost in her mind was the problem of medication and her fear of 'getting it wrong' when Mrs. Quin was on duty. She was obviously lying awake to see who was on night duty, and who would insist on 'three pills at once.'

"I do love the staff... Charley, Hugh, Sarah, Jane, Grace - they're so nice..." she said, "and I *am* happy with them."

I noticed the omission. All because I had failed to persuade the Deputy of the importance of repairing a fractured trust. Why did she seem so dismissive of the impact the incident had had? I didn't know what else I could possibly do to convince her when she herself appeared to believe I was exaggerating the problem, and that it would only be a matter of time before it my girl had forgotten all about it. I would persist.

"Do we need all our rooms Mum?" Minty suddenly asked. And I supposed we could manage with fewer if necessary, and wondered what she had in mind.

"We could bring everybody here to live," she said simply. "Then we wouldn't have to worry about you dying and we'd get lots of help with driving and stuff."

We were back to wanting to create the ideal world, but with no doubt that home was to be the base, and the linchpin.

Though my heart would have none of it, my head told me I was to persevere; to build on the days she enjoyed and the people with whom she was now at ease. But as long as the broken link remained ignored, we would make no progress. Only with that repaired could we concentrate on diet, and other things, one by one. She had lost trust, and worse was fearful. What more serious concern could there be than to believe, rightly or wrongly, that you had been overdosed?

But the lady remained distant, not in an aloof sort of way by any means, but calmly as though benignly tolerating this over attached mother who would eventually realise that others could do it just as well - that they were there to relieve me of responsibility and give me the opportunity to live my own life.

No doubt kindly meant, she had a very long wait! It had been forty years since I had been able to define my own life, and until the

Minty half of me was totally happy and settled, I would remain 'irritatingly attached' and continue to hover stubbornly in the background. She had in fact, on a rare occasion we had conversed, made reference to such a situation, implying they were used to parents who had gone on worrying, failing to notice their offspring had happily 'moved on.'

And so my daughter and I talked the situation through, knowing that every new change needed time; that it was easy to be deflected from the main objective when coping with the differing ways of doing the little things that fill each ordinary day. We would try to accept this. And I knew that with a little support it might have worked, if only self-medication and diet could be re-addressed, and sufficient importance attached to them. Overall there could not have been a finer group of individuals. What they lacked was the finesse facilitated by sensitive daily coordination to enable them to function as an effective, first rate team.

On Saturday she was still tearfully tired and we abandoned the idea of going to the male voice choir concert in the evening - something she normally loves having become familiar with their repertoire – although typically she insisted she would 'love to go for you Mum.' It was clear she just wanted to be at home, to relax without intrusion on our special Saturday candlelit supper. And in the absence of anything on television, we curled into two capacious armchairs, and watched yet again her favourite 'Miracle on 34th Street.'

She awoke refreshed on Sunday, and looking brighter announced she would like to go back for lunch. With my head now spinning in two directions I had to accept the situation might yet be rescued.

On our return, I saw from the display on her bookshelves that she had finished colouring all the large pictures I had brought her last week - designs on white card but with the addition of black furry outlines that gave sharp definition to the shapes. She must have spent hours in her room - but was it because she was bored and they were a way of filling the hours or had she simply enjoyed the time she could give to them, to have done so many?

Was there enough to do here or was it considered that going to the Centre took care of that side of things? I noticed on several occasions she had elected not to go to her Centre and I must ascertain whether due preference, which would be a plus for Greenlands since they had never purported to be other than 'a home,' or because she was too tired to cope with a full day's schedule on insufficient sleep. I had been told during one of my initial visits that residents could, as was their right, 'vote with their feet', and often did, and that always there was someone on duty night and day so that they were never alone, as indeed was so.

She noticed I was admiring her colouring and said, "Will you gets others Mum – the nice man on the market said he would get some new ones soon."

"Good as done," I promised. There wasn't time to say more, for as she was unpacking her bag, a cheerful, breezy young man who may have been a volunteer, popped his head round the door calling, "I've left your lunch on the table!"

She was puzzled, disinclined to rushing of any kind. "They said twelve thirty. It's only quarter past."

She responded as she always does by hurrying to obey and becoming perturbed in the process.

"I'll finish unpacking," I suggested. "You don't want your lunch to go cold."

"Nor the plate," she added sombrely.

I checked the pills in her little wicker box. There was a week's supply but she would be unable to see the labels that had been written in normal sized handwriting. I fished for the black felt tip I always carried in my bag for her, and relabelled them, left a little note apologising but explaining the need to do so, and then went to the kitchen to say 'goodbye'.

Four were tucking enthusiastically into enormous platefuls of beef, roast potatoes, two veg. and Yorkshire puddings. As had been claimed, Sunday lunch at Greenlands was 'something to write home about'.

I planted a kiss on the top of her head and said goodbye, surreptitiously feeling her plate. I didn't want to interrupt, although

126

they were eating silently, all attention on the meal, but with no carer as I had seen on some other Sundays to make the occasion special and to jolly them along. What should have been a companionable group, were instead four individuals who might just as well have been eating alone.

"Plate's cold," she said. "Can you put it in the microwave?"

I looked round and as there was no one to offend by so doing I was able to return her plate to her with the meal as hot as I knew she liked it. "Is everyone else all right?" I asked, and three nodding heads indicated the meal was almost gone anyway, having had a head start on Minty.

"Stay and sit with us," she invited. "Charley and Hugh do."

A dilemma here. I was the 'to be seen and not heard' outsider. How would it be viewed if I were to sit at table with them? But Peter had already pulled out a chair. "For you," he beamed. "You sit next me."

"Well just until one of the staff comes," I agreed.

"Mrs. Quin cooking today," Peter said. "She go to the office when she finished. And William go the other dining room."

Of course the Deputy had administrative matters to attend to, but albeit for good reason, the details that would have made things perfect had again seemed overlooked by the same person. I could understand the pressure to deal with office matters, but their priority did mean that her Sunday lunches might not be the fun that other staff were able to make them. The modest request of a hot plate should have presented no problem and it all added to my gut feeling that my 'very clear notes' had perhaps not inspired concurrence even if they had merited reading.

Rarely over the years have I seen mentally handicapped people motivate each other and yet they respond so happily to company and the conversation of their carers or instructors, looking to them for ideas and fun. Whilst Minty finished her plate - and I cringed at the thought of what the scales would say next morning - we played 'I Spy', but with colours rather than letters and I stayed until their attention was diverted by the arrival of pudding.

"Easy on the custard," I grinned at Minty, who asked what she could have instead. There wasn't an 'instead', and in any case the dessert itself was ultra tempting. Once medication had been resolved, diet must be Battle Mark Two Urgent! Was I being unreasonable and expecting too much? I decided not. Expectation was not at fault having been told that catering was done on an individual basis.

That same evening I received a call 'to let me know that the hundred pounds was almost gone' – just fourteen pounds left -and perhaps I would replenish as soon as possible. Knowing Minty would need only £5 for riding and around £2 for her college lunch before my Thursday visit, I presumed it would be all right if I topped her up then. There seemed no problem with that and when I said I was just a bit surprised the last top up had gone already, the caller suggested I speak with Mrs. Quin about it as she dealt with accounts. She was merely the messenger. It seemed reasonable to ask if I could book a few minutes with her when I called on Thursday.

Perhaps the accounts were what had kept her from having lunch with the residents only hours previously. The time since I last topped up merited further funds on the basis of number of weeks residence, and assuming she had spent all of her sixteen pounds each week, which as far as I was aware she hadn't because I was taking in all she needed. Of course, it must be the hairdos. The more sundries I took in the more was left for visits to the beauty parlour!

Yet again I was plagued by the question of who would help her to budget, to build up a little reserve when I was no longer here. Would she be having expensive hairdos and then buying all her clothes from the charity shops? Nothing wrong with charity outlets - I often popped in and made purchases - but not everything. I printed some sheets detailing my own calculations to compare with theirs. That way both sides could see what I had missed and next time I would leave money before they needed to ask, for I had been embarrassed by the request.

Fumbling my way through my computer course next day, I made little headway for my mind and heart were elsewhere. The phone was ringing as I let myself into the house.

"So, you have freedom to arrange a normal life!" a friend echoed. I smiled wryly. Since Minty had left home, I'd spent every waking hour worrying about being *dead*, never mind having a 'normal life.'

My mind was never away from her, rarely out of earshot of the telephone.

"Fancy going to the Iris Murdoch film?" Carole was continuing. "It's your cup of tea. Why don't we meet for a sandwich and cinema?"

Yes, I would go to the film because I was incapable of shifting my mind from that which obsessed it. But freedom? Was this the nature of it, this mental cage that had me in its grip? I couldn't contemplate going away for a day, much less put an ocean between us to take a holiday, in case there was another problem with medication.

The film did in fact absorb me - not continuously due lapses of concentration, but often enough to follow its thread and appreciate both actors and director.

"There," Carole announced triumphantly. "You *can* do it. It's just a matter of learning to let go - transfer the responsibility. Become your own person."

I looked at her steadfastly. If this was how one of my closest friends saw my situation, how could I criticise the insensitivity of one who barely knew my name? We can all 'let go', however much we are hurting, as long as the one we have released is doing what makes him or her happy. That is after all, the natural way of things.

When I called Minty at six thirty, the world steadied as her voice brought her home again. She was, she told me, due to go out on a group supper on Thursday - a Mexican meal in town.

"Sounds like fun," I said, but she was less excited than when she had been out on her 'one-to-one day,' which apparently could not repeated for some time. The outing then had been with her special carer, but this was for all the residents, and I picked up on the lack of compatibility for her. The fear that had shuddered through me on that first night, resurfaced. I tried hard to raise her enthusiasm and I knew that to please me, she said of course she would enjoy it. It would be fun. And just as I thought she had convinced herself too, she said, 'But it would be nice if you and I could go Mum, and find a special table with a candle.'

Forcing a voice from a tightened throat, it was almost a relief when she reminded me it was time for Emmerdale.

129

"Night Mum. Love you best."

I was a heap of jangled nerves and indecision again. Desolation encased me like a straightjacket. Unable to sleep I made endless cups of tea and told myself repeatedly that I was coping. Must think positively. Yes I was coping. I *was*, wasn't I? I gulped at the tea.   No I wasn't.   I probed first the past, then the future. The one was irrelevant, and the other might never exist.   All I knew was that the present was hell.

CHAPTER THIRTEEN

Wondering if what I was feeling was normal, irrational, something that would pass or remain with me indefinitely, I sought the advice of someone professionally associated with adult learning disability during a lifetime career. To my surprise she didn't offer clichés or comfort, but said unequivocally, "If your instinct says it's not right for her, it's better to say sooner rather than later." She went on to suggest there might be moves to make things better in the future with friendship schemes to run alongside other residential care initiatives. Replacing the receiver, I could feel my emotions settling, my stomach less queasy. I had taken a first step beyond the situation in which I had tossed like laundry in a washing machine for weeks.

I was therefore upturned when, on calling Minty in the evening, a cheerful voice sang, "Peter doesn't want me to go." They had talked about the soaps and knowing each other for 'hundreds of years'. But she must also have talked about leaving for him to have asked her to stay - not something we had done at home, which meant that it was in her head and that she had felt comfortable in discussing it with him. And I saw that if he as another resident could, by chatting, make her feel a sense of belonging, how much more could have been achieved in the same way by a senior member of staff.

Thursday would present the opportunity to mention it again. Meanwhile I had resolved to build on every positive sign and must now draw the mental resources to do exactly that.

"How would you feel about spending the weekend at Greenlands if you and Peter are getting on so well?" I asked.

There was a pause, and then, "*All* weekend?"

"It would give you a chance to find out what they do on Saturdays and Sundays and see if you enjoy it."

"All right," she agreed. "But I'll phone you lots."

"I'll be here," I promised. And to myself added, "Every minute I'll be here. And missing you every single one of them."

In the event, on Thursday neither the pills nor Minty's sundry spending were discussed. Charley was on duty and when I told him I had asked to see the Mrs. Quin for a few minutes, he popped into the office and out again with a single A4 sheet.

"Mrs. Quin left this. It's a list of Minty's weekly expenses."
But why if she couldn't keep the appointment hadn't she said, or was it again a minor matter that didn't merit her time and could equally well be dealt with by another. Was I so irrelevant?

"Thank you," I said, folding the sheet and slipping it into the side pocket of my bag, "but I'd actually asked to have a word. I did make an appointment. I'll come back if it's not convenient."

"Just a tick," he smiled. "Do you want to wait in the dining room a moment?"

When he reappeared, it was with a notebook of figures, dates, and signatures of withdrawals by residents, Minty's included - and an extremely angry manager. It was clear the latter felt insulted and offended, but why? That Charley stayed whilst the anger was sustained when it was not in his nature to do so, gave me the feeling he had been asked to witness anything that was said.

"There has obviously been a misunderstanding," I stammered in the charged atmosphere. "I'd like to know if there are expenses I'm not aware of. I've kept a general tally of her outgoings and would have brought money in if I'd thought she was within the total. I don't like your having to phone for money for I would never let her be short. It would be helpful if we could discuss how often her money will allow visits to the hairdresser and how best to....."

Obviously exasperated, Mr. Brown intervened. 'This was the second time,' I was told vehemently, 'that I'd mentioned hairdressing.' And with that he turned and left.

It was as if my mind no longer had a foothold. I was stunned for this seemed uncharacteristic of him. And was the anger on his behalf or another? And why? Was I really being so irrational? We had established such a good relationship throughout my conversations with him, a relationship that had crumbled in seconds as he pulled the mat from under me. Without his support that had been my anchor, I felt as secure as a flag in a sandcastle

"I don't want to see these," I told Charley. "They are withdrawals by other residents and not my business. I'm only trying to keep ahead and not put you in the position of having to ask for money. I'd hoped to reconcile my figures with yours but........"

"I'm sorry. He probably didn't mean....I'm sure...." He was seeking a way to remain loyal and yet indicate he appreciated my position. "There's obviously a crossed wire somewhere."

I showed him the sheet I'd brought, though for me the figures were racing around the page refusing to be focussed, and he said quietly, "Yes I can see exactly what you mean."
He stopped short of adding that it could all have been so easily sorted, but I could tell that's what he was thinking.

I headed for Minty's room and saw immediately a large, grey metal box sitting on her chest of drawers. Though there was a key in the lock, the box remained unlocked. Lying on the bottom shelf occupying a ridiculously minute portion of it were three strips of pills - now more accessible to a third party than ever they had been when inside the little raffia basket she had kept in her bedside drawer.

Mr. Brown had gone into an office where the all the medicines were kept. I wrote out a cheque for another hundred pounds and placed it on the desk in front of him. It was a strange feeling as if I were approaching a stranger. The bond we had built up throughout the summer meetings had been roughly, irredeemably, and, to me, unnecessarily torn. I needed to get Minty to the hospital for her thyroid test and back again in time for a nap before the Mexican meal that evening, and I made no effort to converse.

Rather more gently than the exercise books had been presented, he handed me an envelope, explaining that it was a copy of a letter from the Housing Officer to me.

"But it's dated two days ago," I began. "I haven't received the original...."

The words fused as my vision blurred. Must get a grip and read it when I got home.

"It's about the rent, and the hundred deposit......but you've just given me a cheque for that......."

He had calmed now, was managing a strained smile in a bid for affability, but I just wanted to get out. It wasn't what he'd said, but how I had felt when he said it.

Drained by the day, I couldn't be bothered with supper, took a couple of biscuits from the tin and looked at the A4 sheet that had been given to Charley to pass on to me. It was a brief routine summary that I imagined each resident had of routine weekly expenses, and which presumably was to explain everything. 'It was 'a plan Minty had agreed to and signed. A plan,' it was stated, 'that is followed correctly, enabling her to attend all her chosen and extra community activities.'

It indicated that outgoings were such as to leave '£2.35 surplus to cover the cost of all toiletries,' (which she had taken from home anyway), 'trips out, haircuts, meals out etc.' And on the basis of that, not only would she need 'topping up' but comparatively expensive trips to the hairdresser would have been out of the question. Significantly, the obvious error hadn't been picked up, again giving me the impression of casual and untroubled oversight of detail.

Although anticipated when she first took up residence, the yoga class had in fact been cancelled since Christmas, leaving only the riding lesson and her subsidised college lunch. Thursday's entry was the blow that winded. It was described as her 'day off from Centre - lunch out with Mum' on which she needed a lunch allowance towards eating out.

At that I couldn't wait to get pen to paper. When I took my girl out to lunch, the cost was mine. Indeed I had always given her some money as I left her so that she would have something in her pocket. But of course that didn't mean she hadn't withdrawn some spending money for the day. I had never asked her. If only we could have talked about it rationally. For the life of me I couldn't understand why such an innocuous conversation had been avoided.

I came to the conclusion that my endeavours to be part of the equation were a nuisance factor to the one, whilst might the other think I was questioning honesty? Surely not? But that might explain the anger. Had I thought them to be dishonest in any way, I would hardly have given my daughter into their care in the first place. Wanting to keep abreast of things and to see where and how she could save a little for when she needed larger items if I were not here to provide them, had been my only objective.

The sheet was only relevant to weeks she attended the Training Centre. As she had gone into residence late in December, had spent eight days at home over Christmas, and then continued the New Year holiday at Greenlands, it hardly reflected a typical weekly expenditure. Not double-checking its accuracy before leaving it for Charley to give to me smacked of cold plates and non-replacement of the 'hospital' mattress. There was a need to talk but I feared my effort to build a comfortable relationship had been misconstrued, and my requests an irritation.

I struggled with the letter all evening, stating that I would be delighted for her to go out for treats - that she could have every penny I owned - but I needed to know how to budget and without a pattern to look at in those early months, I couldn't do so. Indeed if she had had only a couple of pounds left after spending on activities, the hairdressing mentioned would have been impossible, so obviously she *had* built up a reserve which would have tied in with my rough calculations. My enquiry had not been a critical one – merely an attempt to help her to budget for the future when she would be in residence all the time.

I objected to it remaining erroneously on record that I asked my daughter for a contribution for lunch when I took her out and would welcome a note to indicate a correction. I had no other wish than to work in partnership with them, in her interest, but it was clear that such a wish had been misconstrued and that I had well and truly got under someone's skin, whether by giving the wrong vibes, or just being me.

Instinctive initial dislike can, and does happen. Maybe I had unwittingly aroused such sentiment.

I said how much I had appreciated the help and kindness of individual members of staff and drew the letter to a close by apologising for causing offence for none had been intended, and that it concerned me greatly to discover that such tension existed. I checked and re-checked that I had expressed my feelings in the most tactful way, then satisfied I had covered all that was relevant, I sealed the envelope.

I never did receive a reply.

* * *

I wondered how the Mexican meal was going. Minty loved eating out, discovering different décors and atmospheres and I hoped she was enjoying the occasion, totally divorced from the tangles I was trying unravel. I would have been distraught to read the diary I was only allowed to see months later:-

I didn't like the outing. The mex food came on a cold plate and Emily behave badly and shouting. I don't like it when she upset staff. When we got back she shout again. Greg come see. He knocked on her door. Grace come out of Emily's room and give me a hug and said Don't upset. I shooked again in night. Emily came out of her room again late and slammed the door and Grace said Go back to your room but she didn't.'

Imagining her to be happily involved, I cut out shapes from a plastic form of binca and threaded a collection of bulky tapestry needles with varying colours of wool ready for my next visit. It was long after midnight and I was drained. The Housing Officer's letter must wait for the morrow. I would deal with it in the time normally spent driving to the Day Nursery. It was going to be a strange weekend without my constant shadow. Staying at Greenlands for the weekend meant that for the very first time I wouldn't be collecting her from her job tomorrow. She would be in someone else's hands, and at that moment I didn't feel I could bear it.

Looking around a home and garden I had neglected whilst attempting to deal with the concerns at Greenlands and trying to engage with Social Services and bureaucracy in general, there was more than enough to keep me at full stretch for the next month let alone an afternoon. Maybe the misunderstandings would soon be ironed out, the haemorrhaging of energy stemmed, trust established, and all finally running smoothly.

* * *

The strangeness of the letter being a *copy* of one addressed to me when even in this morning's post I had still not received the original, troubled me. Presumably the top copy would have had the Housing Association letterhead and address - absent on the sheet I now held. And more importantly the sender, who, according to the typed name below the space for signature, was that of the Housing Officer with whom I had been dealt with so pleasantly, would have signed it. Having only a 'copy' there was no way of knowing.

Never had I not paid a bill promptly or settled a credit card fully each month. And now, having been told to wait for a bill before making payment, I was asked to pay the rent due to date as soon as possible *'to prevent large arrears accruing.'* The money had been sitting in my bank for that very purpose, awaiting as instructed the receipt of an invoice from the Housing Association. I was incensed.

I was also asked to take sixteen pounds and five pence to Greenlands on a weekly basis from now on, because it had been brought to her attention that Minty had been short of funds and a loan from the housekeeping necessitated. For the hairdo I wondered? I was mortified; felt totally humiliated, and could not equate the tone of the letter with Stephanie. What conversations had taken place to result in such a diametrically opposed attitude?

As I read, and re-read the letter, I began to see how misunderstanding might be occurring, and I felt again that lack of communication, this time between the two people at the top, seemed to be the cause. Mr. Brown had asked me to deposit a hundred pounds at intervals from my own account to cover Minty's personal needs until the deficiency in her allowances had been rectified and which would then form part of the whole sum going direct to Greenlands. Mrs. Quin on the other hand might be unaware of this, and worse, thinking I was withholding some of the amount left for personal expenditure that she felt she should be managing now that my girl was, to quote her words at the time prescriptions were re-directed, 'in their care.' Yet the letter had come from the Housing Officer who knew of the arrangement..... Or had it?

I glanced at the clock. Soon Minty would be saying goodbye to the nursery children. At one minute after mid-day, she would go out to the car park to meet not me, but the member of staff who was to collect her and for the first time, instead of coming home, she would go back to Greenlands.

At twelve twenty five my phone rang and a distressed voice was saying, "Mum, no one's here for me. I've come back into the office. I can't see Joe. He brought me this morning but I can't find his red car now."

"Stay right there," I told her. "Is Mrs. Mann with you?"

"No, she's gone to the Bank cos she thought I was leaving."

I kept her talking for five minutes and then suggested she went out to look again. If no-one was there she must come back into the office, sit by the phone, and I would call her. While she checked, I ran to the garage and pulled the car out into the drive. I could be there in twenty minutes. A young classroom assistant answered my call and looked out of the window when I asked if Minty had been collected.

"No, no ....I can see her coming back to the office. Oh, she's turning round again. She's getting in a black car..."

I urged her to rush outside. "It should be a red one. Don't let her get in it if there's any doubt. I'll come and get her."

"It's a lady....she appears to know her... Mrs. Mann's just driven in. She's going up to them now. She's saying something to the lady."

I calmed. Of course it needn't be the same driver who collected her. Stupid of me, but had they not told her who would be coming and what colour car to look out for? And the driver should have got out of the car to look for *her*, given her limited eyesight; something else I had explained in detail in the letter I had left with them on that first day.

"They've gone now. Mrs. Mann's coming back to the office. Do you want to hold?"

"She hasn't been the same," Mrs. Mann said. "It's not working. She's absolutely drained - too tired even to joke with me."

"Has she talked to you?"

"Not much – no energy. Says she loves....." And she reeled off the names she had been told. The same ones Minty always included to me.

"She did tell me about the pills," she added.

Proof that bridge building had been essential; that it hadn't been an unreasonable request, and what I felt to be reluctance to do so had left her feeling afraid and vulnerable.

"There's no bubble any more. The two of you have become a unit. It's how everybody thinks of you. And I know I'm not renowned for my tact, but you looked ninety when you dropped her off last week."

"You mean I've left it too late."

"I don't mean anything. Nothing's the same. It isn't right."

So it wasn't just me being an irritating mother. At last I had an impartial point of view from someone outside the situation who could see at first hand. She had clarified my resolution. The letter was now merely a practical job to be done; no longer an emotional ripping apart. I didn't even rush to catch the afternoon's post, but left it lying like a corpse on the desk.

A corpse, because it couldn't hurt any more.

Her diary much later revealed Minty's version of events:
Joe took me to my nursery job. He is nice. I went to the car park but he not there. I go to the office and phoned my Mum. She said to stay. She will fetch me. Mrs Mann come back and say I will come with you to look. She was bit cross with lady. She come in black car. And she say she been waiting in her car. I was frightened they not come.

The weekend was long, and we phoned and chatted often.

"Are you going to have a candlelight supper?" she asked on Saturday morning after her breakfast, and I was about to say, "Not by myself," but that might have influenced her reaction, so I said, "Maybe. What are you planning? Are you going out with anyone today?"

"Don't think so. I spect I'll just do some pictures. There aren't any barns like at Home Farm where I can go and do things. I'll come home next Saturday."

"If you want to."

"I do. You have a candlelight supper tonight and call me. Call me when the candle is still flaming."

"I promise."

And then without any warning, she asked ponderously, "Mum, in your 'pinion, am I the oldest of your children?"

I responded with a suitable pause as if giving the question the serious thought it merited. "Yes, I do believe you are."

"So that means I do the best thinking then?"

"Go on."

"I'm going to ask you a big question. Are you ready?"

"Fire away!"

"Right." And I heard the intake of breath that always prefaced something she felt to be significant or world shattering. But I could not have been prepared for the question that followed.

"When will you be *nearly* dead?"

"That's a hard one."

"I know. So think carefully."

It's an odd sensation to hear one's own choice of phrase coming out of the mouth of an offspring.

"I'd have to make a guess. I can't work it out exactly."

"But you don't *feel* nearly dead?

"No. No I don't." On Thursday I did, I thought to myself, but not now, not any more.

"Good. I had an idea. Are you concentrating?"

"Tell me."

"Let's stay together until you're *nearly* dead, and *then* I'll leave home. It's very precious being together isn't it?"

It was. So precious I didn't want to waste another second like this.

"You know why we tried sweetie, don't you?"

"So when you're dead I'll be safe."

"We'll see Saturday and Sunday through, and both have a really long think and then try to make the best decision."

140

And I knew, as I had known on the first night, that though the staff were as wonderful a group as could be found anywhere, I had not found the right place for her. There was care and compassion in full measure, and she was comfortable and secure with almost all of them, but however strong the chain they made, one broken link had devalued their total input. And now it seemed a working relationship to repair that crack, was out of reach.

Above all she needed activity and to be motivated, not just cared for, however lovingly. And most crucially, to continue the independence we had built up over the years at home. It was unfortunate that her Centre, now itself thrown into a period of change and stringency, was currently failing to provide all she had enjoyed in the past.

In earlier years she had looked forward to each day's activities - swimming, riding, cooking and bowling etc. But as a group of parents we all knew what was, or rather what would not be in store when the Training Centre was renamed 'Resource' Centre. With that change of nomenclature went also a number of valued members of staff. Committed, quality staff who obviously felt their services were undervalued, a fact evidenced in the restructuring of salary scales and job titles. Whilst they, and those in their charge, were fulfilled and active, Minty would come home tired but content and happy. Now she was looking for the motivation she lacked in the daytime. Greenlands was not, however, set up to assume a dual role and provide activities that were increasingly cut from the Centre.

Above all she was tired. Uncannily tired. A light sleeper, she was most affected by her companion's door slamming and noisy outbursts, none of which poor Emily could help, and which indicated *her* very special needs. Even without the hindsight later afforded by the diary, I knew the situation could not continue. But she had thrown me in the past by being suddenly revived by input from a staff member. We must put the coming weekend to the test for their sake as well as ours.

She called again after supper. "I'm going to do my big think now," she said. "But a new think won't come. It's the same think. We're perfect 'panions aren't we Mum?"

"When other people come on duty, you might find yourself thinking differently," I said. "It happens sometimes. Just take things very slowly. And if you aren't sure, then we'll wait some more."

"Ok Love you Mum. I'll try. Call me in the morning."

With a great lump of lead where my heart should have been I wondered if those involved had any idea what the change to our lives after over forty years, was taking out of us. I settled again to formulate my reply to the Housing Officer, and discovered that the 'lump of lead' could do a pretty good imitation of thumping.

I explained that though I had been given a copy of her letter on Thursday, I had not yet received her signed top copy. It was now Saturday. As I had phoned her only recently to say that in the continued absence of an invoice, I was putting money aside in the bank, I was surprised to receive the demand, but more affected by the impression she must have gained that had prompted her to write it. There was no point in qualifying, because what followed must be the result of our decision tomorrow.

I remembered the year I'd had a very disturbed little boy in school and on one occasion had given him a large paintbrush, correspondingly huge sheet of paper and encouraged him to paint to music. The calm we achieved was significant. Well the teacher must now become the pupil. Impulses springing from loneliness are powerful and recognising how chewed up I was, I went to the garage via the tiny covered area where we often ate outside, and which was black and white like the rest of the house. A tin of tuscan bronze that had sat in the garage for years would give it an Italian feel, especially if I painted the shutters green.

It was way after dusk in mid-winter, hardly the time to be starting outside decorating. But I wasn't decorating a house. I was trying to repair the crumpled mess that was me for these days I was experiencing sensations I couldn't logically explain. Doubtless I would be horrified next morning at the bits I'd missed and the edges I'd fudged. No matter; I needed to swish paint. I rigged up an inadequate electric light and set to. The air was keen and I shivered as I finished the first coat by moonlight. If anyone came now they'd have me sectioned.

I told Minty about it next morning. "It's orange," I said, for 'tuscan' would mean nothing to her. "And I'll make a green checked tablecloth....."

She stopped me abruptly. "That's where we'll eat when I come home," she said.

"You've done your thinking?"

"Yes. Same think. I like you and me best."

* * *

My fault. Checking should have been even more thorough, more circumspect. I had no illusions about the potential problems that might result from a decision to terminate the current agreement. Bridges might be burned irreparably, the 'system' upset. But my brain was no longer in charge; had in fact abandoned me.

Emotions had taken over and were telling me that all we could be sure of was Today. We make plans for the future, think we have learned from the past, and dismiss the present as if it is but a means to an end instead of the 'here and now' to be enjoyed as the most valuable thing we have.

CHAPTER FOURTEEN

With the letter sealed, some of the weight that had oppressed me fell away. There was no point in posting it for the review was only a couple of days away. In it I had asked to be invoiced for the bed, should the next resident require the hospital type one it had replaced, and for the medicine box that had at last appeared. I wished to pay for both given that they had been purchased expressly for my daughter. I stressed that lovely as the home and staff were, Greenlands had not proved to be the right place. My mistake: no one else's.

That done, I phoned the longstanding friend to whom we made an annual summer visit, and who had spoken with me many times during the course of the past debilitating weeks. Characteristically, and before I could tell him of my decision, he expressed his own, 'having thought much on the matter.'

"As I see it, in order to protect a future of indeterminate length or brevity, indeed may never happen, we have two people who are existing rather than living, taking no joy in the present, and in danger of becoming sufficiently ill as to minimise the possibility of longevity. Um."

I had expected him to follow with a lengthy discourse when I told him of developments. Instead he said succinctly, "Good. Now go and have a brandy and get some rest woman!"

* * *

Arrangements for the review were rushed through. When I made the routine phone call next evening, Minty said that Greg had told her about it, and that she could choose whether to take the day

144

off from the Centre or be collected at lunchtime. It came as a surprise that she would be present, for I had imagined a meeting with Mr. Brown and the Social Worker in the way we had met prior to her admission. But of course the situation had changed. Whereas I had been important enough to be included whilst she lived at home, now I was an appendage whose view, alongside those 'now in charge of her care' would be considered.

Wanting to spare her any hint of the atmosphere that pertained, I wrote another letter addressed to Social Worker, Housing Officer, Manager and Deputy, expressing regret, and taking full responsibility for not realising that without more compatible companionship, she was unlikely to settle. We had decided she would cease to be a tenant. I would take that, and copies of the letters I had written in the past few days, and deliver them personally before Minty could be involved. Given the pressures, especially on the Social Worker, I could at least save their time should they then prefer that the meeting did not go ahead. But wheels had been set in motion..... It would probably take another meeting to cancel this one.

In the event it was three o'clock before Minty came in because the decision was debated for an hour, not by the three of us as I had anticipated, but what appeared to my strained nerve, an intimidating roomful. Mr. Brown made clear his opinion I was making a mistake - that he had known it take three years for someone to settle. The Social Worker who had arrived late was initially cross I had taken such a decision without discussing it with her beforehand, but mellowed as I presented my case, and I sensed our earlier cordiality return for a while. I thought of the times I had left messages for her via the office, and the lack of responses. As for 'three years to settle,' no one was going to take such an experimental period from my daughter's life. They were all looking at the situation objectively; appearing to me so sure of their own infallibility.

With heart throbbing, I sat as part of the semi circle whilst an empty chair facing us had obviously been placed there for Minty. Stephanie, the Housing Officer said gently that it was clear the letter sent to me about money had caused hurt and offence, and I noticed she said 'the' and not 'her' letter. And then my correspondence and decision were set aside like 'any other business,' and it was insisted we continued with the review as it should have been conducted had my pre-emptive decision not upset matters.

Everyone became more at ease as they reverted to the anticipated and politically correct format. We had structure; an agenda to follow. So much less trying than an irritating mother with an over active imagination.

I heard how she had settled in happily and had a close friend in Peter; that she enjoyed the candlelight dinner, got on well with staff, and had fun installing her new bed when it arrived. In line with the set procedure, a member of staff was asked to comment on her own observations, and I noticed it was the newly promoted young woman selected to replace Charley, who had been chosen. She was hardly likely to tread on anyone's toes and agreed she hadn't heard any disturbance that might deprive Minty of sleep. And Jane, her special carer for whom this was her first such meeting, was too shy to do other than absorb the format. None of the many staff with whom I had had such easy, relaxed conversations was there. I was alone with my 'hang-ups.'

Now Minty was to be invited in, and so long having been spent on my concerns, I was requested not to speak during her presence but to let her have the floor. It was after all what *she* felt that mattered.

In the event she was more successful than I in achieving an awareness of 'anything she wasn't happy with,' though the Social Worker quite rightly asked many questions to satisfy herself that I hadn't influenced her. Reciting the now familiar list of staff, she thought they were all 'kind and lovely.' She had been very frightened when it was insisted she had the pills all at once when she went to work; didn't like being 'waked' up in the night by the shouting and banging, and had decided to come home and they were all very welcome to come and visit whenever they liked.

There were concealed smiles at her choice of words, but she had had an effect. She left the room and the review was at an end. The weight of all the things left unsaid bore down on me like a storm cloud.

146

The Social Worker declared she would go and see Minty alone. I wanted to beg her to understand that if someone has cared for another 24/7 for forty plus years, the handicapped person will have superseded all else in the carer's life. The carer will feel bereft not only of her charge, but of her own identity and purpose when the need for such care is no longer there. She'll be as fragile as an empty shell without the substance inside that over the years has become a reason to be. And worse she will be rendered too raw and empty to recognise or explain the logic of her emotion.

But that doesn't mean she has lost her reason. Knowing she herself has requested intervention, she will try to justify action and reaction. Emptied of all that was her purpose, she now desperately needs to have a link with those to whom she has entrusted the most precious gift. But of course this is real social work with the need to listen, and for which there seems no time in today's world of crisis management.

Long ago she may have railed at such a responsibility, yearned to live her life the way she planned, but gradually over time, and certainly if the caring was done out of love not duty, the commitment will have *become* the life. With or without realising it, her own life will have been put on hold much as with any young mother whilst her children are small. In the case of Down's however, childhood is for life. There is no maturing into true adulthood. As for the depth of love, draw the analogy of telling a couple celebrating not only a golden wedding but fifty years of being a unit, that just in case one of them dies tomorrow, it would be a good idea to move into a separate dwellings today. If both were still active and healthy nobody in their right mind would suggest such a thing. Better let Nature take its course.

That was the strength of emotion being subjected to change, and the carer surely merits being an equal part of the equation. For those whose inclusion was motivated by an apparent need to 'come to the rescue,' this may come as a surprise. It is none the less a fact. Ignore it and you are building on sand.

And of course Social Services had indeed entered the situation at our request. And if I could not have envisaged the emotional fall out or the intense psychological impact, how on earth, unless they had experienced it all before, could I expect them to have foreseen it? No, the error and responsibility were mine.

* * *

I was left in a shameful state with the Housing Officer, the only person with whom I seemed to have empathy at that moment. She understood completely how worried I must have been about the lack of a diet specifically requested by the hospital, but urged me to be strong, and repeat my concerns. She was sure it could all be put right. But I had no strength or courage left; no more resources to call on. Nor did I share her conviction. As for airing my concerns, God knows I had tried. But as with so much modern practice, it seemed the only time to register concern effectively was when remarks could be minuted, and reports compiled and distributed to 'interested parties' who by then of course would have moved on to another day and another crisis.

For no special reason I thought of a young man in 'community care' whose washing machine failed to function. From what I heard the situation was noted, a report made and circulated, the correct procedures followed and in due course, after three weeks, the machine was repaired. But what of the hours and days comprising those three weeks for the person most affected? Few mentally handicapped people have a sense of time - it's either immediate or long. And length equates to worry and uncertainty.

There was nothing now beyond this terrible weariness. Nothing left over of me even to worry about the future. I had wanted so desperately - and presumably as any other single ageing parent in the same position - to have the ties cut gently; to be kept involved and to feel I was still part of her life whilst making the future safe. To work together with the team to whom I had entrusted her, through a transition period *for both*, to ensure her stability and happiness. For it to be acknowledged that forty plus years of caring surely constituted enough experience to make a contribution. That it was not enough to say 'Come and see her whenever you like;' but for it to be accepted that it was impossible not to feel an integral part of her life until she signalled she was flying without help. With confidence and trust now shattered, I felt only isolation.

The bond wasn't an umbilical cord that could be cut and discarded. It wasn't ours to sever. And I needed them to understand this. She wasn't just any tenant looking for somewhere to live and from whom it could be assumed she would find her own way to settle. When the Manager had walked out of the kitchen that day, he had, for me at least, broken the thread that had held us together as a team who cared for her, and had left me tossing on the current with no anchor.

* * *

The Social Worker returned. "Your daughter says she wants to think it over a bit longer. I'll come and see her next week."
And I could not help thinking how much fear could have been avoided if she had spared half an hour earlier for such a visit. She would surely have had more success as an official, unemotionally involved third party in persuading of the need for bridge building. I supposed we were now the 'crisis that required management.' Was it *so* unreasonable to have wanted intervention *before* crisis?

I went to Minty's room. She was lying on her bed, tearful.

"I told her I'd think again," she said. And I knew, because her every response and reaction was second nature to me that she would have given the reply she thought was expected of her. Knew too that had I told them that, no one in the present atmosphere would have believed me, even though it had been put it in writing for them on her first day. I was now the impossible mother who couldn't let go.

And yes, as long as she needed my support, a rottweiler had nothing on me. Unless and until she was happy. Then I'd need no one, no one in the world to persuade me to release her. I would watch her fly and my heart would sing for her for I would have achieved the ultimate ambition of any parent, that of seeing an offspring grasping life with all the confidence in her own ability to enjoy it.

I held her hand, needing to relieve her wretchedness, and saw she had done some packing. I wondered if the Social Worker had noticed the suitcase.

149

"Do you *want* to think again?" I asked softly. "Remember, whatever you want to do is fine. I'll go and sort it."

"No. I want to come home, but not tonight. I'd like to say goodbye to...." and out tumbled the familiar names. "I don't know when they'll come on duty. It might be one of the next days."

"Shall we go and make a cup of tea?"

She nodded and we went to the kitchen. It was obvious I was being given a wide berth by staff who had been in the meeting, though ones unaffected by the afternoon smiled as warmly as usual as they came and went about their duties. I stayed long enough that if the senior staff had wanted to say anything else to me they had opportunity to do so. But as we heard the sounds of supper, I let myself out feeling surreptitious, and as welcome as a burglar. I promised Minty I'd visit again tomorrow. All sensible attitudes were now on hold.

"Phone tonight," she said. As it was now almost six I would call immediately after Coronation Street. It had been one hell of a day.

When I did, she told me she was feeling better and that Jane had chatted with her in her room and had hugged her and said that if only she could change her room so that she would be able to sleep properly, she would do so. I knew Jane would be feeling she should have challenged the assertion that the nocturnal noise had caused no problems, and I would have assured her that I had understood her nervousness. As the new girl, she couldn't. In any case her silence had been no less ineffective than my earnest statements. I was just grateful for her kindness to my girl. There was no way the bedroom situation could be changed given the physical layout of the house. And in any case that wasn't the only problem, as we both knew.

Minty was obviously very fond of her special carer and I must support her and be watchful for any eleventh hour change of heart. With attention to details that were fundamentally important to her however inconsequential to others with a wider perspective, it could all have been so different. In a world where parameters are so narrow, perceptions, little things, are more significant; small daily happenings that can make life spectacular or miserable.

It is a development of today's society. We don't listen enough to the person central to the exercise; the one who can supply all the clues needed to achieve objectives. The focus is on 'criteria', making reports, meeting targets, complying with politically designed rules to fit the mass and tailored to fit no one in particular. Conclusions are drawn from surveys; computer-generated, box-ticking assignments that turn us all into grey characterless nonentities. That way we fit into compartments so much more conveniently.

* * *

Too fraught to tackle any of the jobs needing attention, I phoned Jeannie because I needed confirmation I'd done the right thing in meeting them head on this afternoon. She hesitated, and then said she'd been reluctant to influence me at a time that could provoke damaging reactions, but now the gentle tenor of her voice echoed our Welsh friend's uncompromising sentiments. She could, she said, have told me weeks ago that it wasn't going to last.

Another friend urged caution. "You'll never get the place back again," he warned. "Think what you're doing."

But I wasn't doing anything at this moment. Fate itself had decreed a delay.

Before I collected her for the weekend, I summoned the last mental and physical effort to contact the Social Worker again. Would she now grant the request I had made some weeks ago to talk over events? Perhaps together we could meet with the Manager and Deputy and discuss the promises that had been given seemingly in good faith, and then broken in the name of 'policy.' If some bridge building and reassurance could be guaranteed, if we could impress on them the serious effect of the pills, I was prepared to hold fire on my decision *if* Minty herself was entertaining any doubt. But she wasn't in the office, and though I left several messages, none was returned. I would try again on Monday.

Again Minty slept for much of Saturday and Sunday until the white face resumed its natural pallor, and the red eyes were less sore. I cooked her a weight-watcher's stir-fry for lunch when she declined to go back for Sunday roast, and telephoned to say she would return in the early evening.

I tossed events and possibilities around for most of the night. Would for instance, all still be in place for her to resume her previous arrangements to go to the same Centre she had continued to attend whilst at Greenlands, if indeed the decision to come home was made. First things first: I must try the Social Worker's number again as soon as the office opened in the morning. But the secretary informed me that the she was not expected in the office all day. I left another message explaining the need to speak as soon as possible. If she made contact with her secretary, the message would be passed on.

In the event, I had more success in speaking with the duty manager at the Training Centre. There might be a problem with transport on one of the days, but we could just switch her day off. Otherwise the original service, in the event of course of it becoming necessary, could be resumed. Neither of us prolonged the conversation and I promised to be in touch whatever the outcome.

I decided that if I finally made contact with the Social Worker, I would ask if I could be present when she visited Minty. I would sit in the background and remain silent, but I'd know whether her responses were genuinely felt, or just said to please. And that knowledge in itself would help to confirm, or not, the reliability of the decision expressed at the review.

I wrote out some simple and quick menu suggestions as alternatives for the jacket potatoes, which might prove helpful to young, particularly male, staff. Minty had made them with me at home and they might like to involve her in the preparation. Though as yet it hadn't happened, that was what I had been given to understand during those summer meetings, would be the case. Now of course, I could see the practical difficulties in that there had to be an individual diabetic menu for one resident, and time might not allow for a second one.

Nevertheless I had been told that meeting individual's dietary needs was 'the policy,' and as such was one of the factors that persuaded me this would be the right place for her. I enlarged the font to do second copies that Minty would be able to see, and put them all in an envelope for the morrow. If we could get this right, maybe, just maybe, other problems could also be resolved.

I was ill prepared for the Social Worker's reaction next day. No, she would not like me to be there when she visited Minty. And what was the point of her going anyway when I had already made up my mind? I was stunned. How and why had she jumped to this conclusion having been instrumental in delaying our decision? Mystified, I made no instant comment and I heard that she had been out of the office of the previous day when I phoned because she was at the Centre; was in fact with the duty manager when I had made the call re transport.

That she had misread to my call, or possibly only overheard a part of the response to it, and then, not unreasonably in the circumstances, put two and two together and made five, was plain. The receiver was replaced cutting off further exchange, and with that the last shred of my resolve disintegrated as I tried to make sense of the sequence of events.

The question that must be asked when I could finally set them aside, was unequivocally, 'Did we know without a single doubt that we had found the right place for her to be when I was no longer here? On her own, without me to visit, and no family in the area, was it the place where she could be fulfilled and happily occupied around the clock? And was it right to go on doing something just because I wasn't strong enough to hold out against its imposition on me? I couldn't know, but the answer was only minutes away.

Replacing the receiver, my legs were rooted to the ground. If she were convinced she had the facts, she would certainly have alerted Greenlands. I jumped as the phone rang. That would be Mr. Brown now. But it wasn't. It was Minty calling from the Centre at tea-break.

"Hello Mum. Love you." And then she said abruptly, and as if suddenly relieved of indecision, "I want to come home because I like our lives together. I like our talking. I like all the things we do and the places we go. I miss answering the phone and telling you the messages that people give and I love the nice suppers and friends coming and laughing. And I like polishing things and making them shine and you saying I'm much better than you. And I like our plannings. And I want to be with you for hundreds of years."

It all came rushing out like a tornado. An avalanche that told me she was valuing 'Today'; settling for *quality* of life as she perceived it; a life of doing and being needed. At her own level, she had assessed, and reached a decision. Whilst each of our perceptions of quality is different, she was saying that she wanted to seize every moment, really see it and live it as she wished, and enjoy - not in the future but *now*.

"Then I'd better call and tell them," I heard myself saying, and to myself added, "although it would seem as if they've already been informed."

I did exactly that. It was time to come home. Whether my heart or head was telling me, I had no notion. But Minty knew. I called and said that in the circumstances I would like to collect her the day after tomorrow. On Thursdays Mr. Brown had always been in the office and it was courteous that he should have the opportunity to say anything to me that he felt to be outstanding.

"I'm not sure ......," Mrs. Quin began hesitantly.

"I shall pay the rent for the whole period of notice," I assured her. "And anything else that is due."

Satisfied that rules would be met, she said perfectly pleasantly, and with absolutely no indication of ill-feeling, "That's fine then."

She hadn't said that she would be sorry to lose us, or was sad that things hadn't gone to plan, and I wondered if she were thinking merely, 'win some, lose some,' for nothing else had seemed to me to ruffle her. Perhaps she was just glad to be rid of me for we had never achieved a rapport. I suspected the Manager would be more affected; would feel regret that he was losing a client, and I wanted to be able to thank him, withdraw amicably, and set aside our recent, and only disagreement.

I telephoned the Housing Officer and asked her to send the bill for all the things I'd mentioned in my letter of last week and whatever rent I owed in lieu of notice.

"What a pity," she said. "It needn't have been like this. So unfortunate."

Minty was anxious to know if I had spoken with them, and I told her of my intention to collect her on Thursday. I hoped that would give her time to speak with the members of staff she was close to. I decided not to ask her if the Social Worker had chatted with her at the Centre. Best leave things alone now.

CHAPTER FIFTEEN

I breathed deeply as I pulled into the car park. I would not appear broken whatever was said, but remain calm and accept that were I in the Manager's position, I too would feel upset. I had wasted their time and effort, and must accept the resulting acrimony. And above all, I must avoid Minty being involved for she was acutely aware of atmosphere even when not understanding the nature of it. But Mr. Brown's car wasn't there; maybe he would come shortly. I tapped on the office door and was acknowledged as evenly as if I were on a routine visit.

"I'll get the balance of your last deposit with us whilst you collect her things," Mrs. Quin said pleasantly.

Minty was in the kitchen with Joe at the very spot he had patted her shoulder when I had left her on the first night. There was something poignant about that, and despite my resolve to maintain composure, I was unable to say anything of any consequence and just nodded and smiled.

"Take care of yourselves," he said gently. "Great pity. These things happen sometimes."

I suggested that the two continued to have coffee together whilst I loaded the car, but characteristically he insisted on helping me.

Each time we took something out to the boot, I expected Mr. Brown's car to appear until it dawned that he might have *chosen* not to be there. Mrs. Quin would probably phone him when we had left, and I was out of the way. That saddened me for I would have preferred to set our differences aside before leaving.

I sought Jane but she wasn't on duty, so I asked Joe to tell her I would have liked to say goodbye properly. I left a card in the office to thank the staff for everything they had done and wished there had been an opportunity to explain. To those with no knowledge of the events of recent days, Minty's departure would seem precipitate to say the least. To Mrs. Quin I expressed regret that things had worked out as they had, and for the first time I caught a glimmer of a suggestion that she was thinking she might just have misjudged me. The time and opportunity had passed, and unceremoniously we slipped through the front door.

Strangely in the numbness that was taking hold I could only think that the funeral form she had given to me on that first night, had never been requested. Details had been asked of me; the law had been complied with. In any case the onus was on me to hand it in, if only I had been able to address it.

My hands shook as I reversed out of the parking space. I hadn't wanted to end things like this with the Manager obviously avoiding an encounter. We needed to have closure, amicably, for I thought highly of Greenlands and felt that had he been there on the day to day basis I had understood would be the case, all could have worked out differently. There was guilt attached now and instead of the elation I had expected to feel, I was trembling.

"Aren't you very well Mum?"

"I will be when we get home."

"When I make you a frothy coffee like always?"

"Like always. Yes that would be so nice."

Leaning her head on my shoulder, she seemed to understand that loss of composure could only be a temporary state because I had to find a way for us to get on with our lives again. In the end, the decision, though traumatic, hadn't been difficult; indeed the very person who had opposed it, finally pushed me into it. The execution of it left me feeling inadequate and insecure.

* * *

As with all changed human situations, there would be questions and comments to deal with, as indeed proved to be the case. Opinions were expressed openly or indirectly, gently or forcefully. Some used the benefit of hindsight, whilst others reiterated previously stated opinions. She had after all been warm and well cared for, living in a perfectly clean, pleasant and healthy environment..... well-fed if not with the attention to her specific needs that she and I would like. Carers as a group were superb, the best I had come across anywhere, and if there was weakness, I had thought it to be a lack of cohesion and communication from the top.

Friends were tactfully non-committal and whilst some had thought she should never have left home in the first place, others considered I hadn't given it long enough. I had been too soft and could only blame myself if she were suddenly left alone. I had blown my chance - made the decision too hurriedly. One, doubtless with the intention of firing my addled brain into facing reality, referred to our situation, then immediately regretted doing so, as 'a life sentence.'

"For God's sake, when do you have a life of your own?" she demanded.

One learns over the years to remain silent rather than explain to a mind already made up. In any case I had no will for such a task.

"That wasn't why we did it," was all I could manage.

* * *

Guilty? Yes on all counts. Guilt is never far away. I hadn't been able to see it through. Heaven knows I had tried, but nothing could have prepared me for the buffeting onslaught to my senses. Tossed by doubt and emotional upheaval, *I simply did not cope.*

Understandably my critics were looking from the other side of the fence. All the factors they raised were the 'big screen'; the view that was so reasonable from the onlooker's standpoint. It's a medley of tiny things that make up life's quality. My girl had lacked sufficient compatible companionship and as anyone seeking to share an apartment, or enter a relationship will testify, this is the most important consideration. To live at the Ritz with someone whose company you constantly try to avoid cannot compare with being in a humble room with another whose company is a pleasure and with whom you feel utterly at ease.

She had needed friends with whom she could chat, girlie-fashion, sitting on each other's beds, rather than depend on carers for this; wonderful carers who could spend *some* time but not as much as a friend given that they had other less able residents to deal with. She needed motivation and activity instead of sitting for hours in her room; gaps I could fill to a lesser extent whilst still alive and able to visit her, but afterwards - and it was the 'afterwards' I was trying to safeguard, - it was not the life that would most fulfil her.

So, back to not being able to die knowing she was all right, and all involved would have been justified in declaring that a self inflicted wound. However, for now, we had decided not to trade the present for a future that may or may not happen. I know this could be seen as ungrateful, uninformed and misguided by those in charge of spreading the little there was from social service budgets, but with respect few of them had lived it.

If I was asking too much, it was a measure of my love for her, and because she was *worth* the best. I couldn't ask them to realise the marvel of her nature. Only by adoring her as I do could they know and understand what the effort had cost. In the end I had allowed instinct to be my guide and if I needed confirmation we had made the right decision, it came from several diary entries shown to me many, many weeks after her return home.

'At home I lay lots of pretty tables for us to have candlelight dinner but here we just put a mat and cutlery for each of us. I miss making the table look pretty with red candles and napkins and wineglasses.'

'Sometimes we have Orient Express supper at home because to celebrate mum's retirement, we went on the Orient Express for a day and had champagne-breakfast and a waiter served our dinner and we sat in chairs with wings on top like we have at home in the little room where we watch TV. So we put supper on a tray and sit in our chairs and take turns to be the waiter for each other and we have Bucks Fizz and laugh when it bubbles over the top of the glass.'

And when I wake up in the morning, mum comes in to give me a cuddle and say I love you.
And sometimes we get Chinese supper and share it on special plates hot, not just warm.

'I missed all mum's hugs and us bopping around the kitchen and friends coming to supper and making it special for them. And mum she goes downstairs to make cup of tea and see the house is nice and warm and then I go down and we have breakfast together. She taught me how to make porridge with her and says I make it best of all – no lumps. I tried to make it here but it went wrong and I made too much and couldn't eat it.

Dumbly, and on the basis of getting back on the horse after taking a tumble, I rang Home Farm. There was neither will nor strength to try again, but I felt an overwhelming need to tell someone I'd got it wrong.

"Join the human race," a comforting voice consoled. "People often try several residences before feeling they've found the right one. Best if it can be avoided of course, but not always possible."

During the conversation I was advised to see how things would go over a couple of years. Government directives were causing charities to rethink strategies and criteria. It could be that only the most severe cases would have access to the tiny on-site bungalows Minty had once set her heart on. Changes were afoot, and reorganisation inevitable. It would be well to let the dust settle for a while, for both of us. She couldn't know, but letting the dust settle was all I was capable of just now.

Self-reproach was inevitable and depression had me in its grip. Suffocating guilt and the fear I may not outlive her became a living nightmare. Though well intentioned, the attempt had been abortive, and the after-effects long lasting. The social worker disappeared from our horizon like vapour; not surprisingly my letter of thanks, and regret, was ignored. I couldn't discuss, redeem, or close the situation, and I moved in a vacuum as I struggled to find the way forward. It was as if all the people involved were characters on a stage, but that we, not they, had ceased to exist.

Hollow and insecure, I felt confidence ebbing further and further away. I got through the days in a dim-witted trance, putting

160

on a performance for the one person to whom I must always appear to be in control. Only by absorbing myself into the routine of getting her to her venues and caring for her needs could I find the means of simply continuing to exist, as a swarm of uncertainties punctuated each day. I feared life's fragility, and the brevity of time remaining. With a body drained of strength, and a mind of resolution, I fumbled blindly for a way ahead.

Our long-standing friend in Wales had learned that he now suffered from a degenerative condition. He would not, he told me, wait for it to render him immobile or dependent on others. And most certainly he would not enter a nursing home 'to go rotten' and would choose his own way to go. I suspected the morphine that was prescribed to reduce his pain would be instrumental in his demise. There was no gainsaying him though numerous friends tried. He insisted he had had a good life and would end it whilst he had the power and the means to do so rather than settle for half an existence.

I pondered his situation and wondered if he had now given me the answer in this solitary night of doubt and despair. If I too lost the ability to care for my daughter; became dependent on others, could I find the courage to end it for both of us before life became intolerably confusing for her.

Our friend would be taking his own life; to follow that particular path on another's behalf would be the ultimate crime. Nightmares can be mass-produced by a troubled mind, especially one in a tunnel. There had to be another way. And I was not going to find it by knocking the hell out of myself. From somewhere I must find the means to pick myself up and carve a life for the two of us.

If anyone needed proof of the bond, I would suggest listening to a Classic FM presenter who telephoned one evening to tell me he would read the letter he had received from my daughter on the following Sunday programme. I had found her writing laboriously at the dining table for well over an hour one morning, and making our elevenses, asked her what such an important job could be.

"Secret," she said, with an air of satisfying finality. "There I've finished. Now I need the selotape."

"For a letter?"

"Yes, 'cos I want you to post it but you mustn't look inside. I can't do the envelope. Please send it to Nick Bailey."

She thrust several sheets of folded A4, heavily sealed around each edge, into my hands. Written at such cost, I hadn't the heart to refuse, and together we walked down the lane to the post box. I imagined her letter would be put into a bin on arrival, for it would take a degree of patience to decipher her inimitable spelling without even the aid of punctuation.

And so I was overwhelmed by the compassion behind his telephone request to help with some of the words. Beyond that he would tell me nothing except that *Bruchs* was spelt Brooks, and that she had written 'lovely' with a long wavy line between the 'l' and the rest of the word, so that was how he would say it! I must listen on Sunday. I confess to some apprehension at the thought of what he might have been told for amused friends have many times said that it's as well I'm not a scarlet woman for they hear all that I do and everywhere I go!

This was what I heard over the air that day.

One day my mum said let's make a special cake for your birthday. But we had a power cut in the middle and it all went wrong so mum gave it to the birds. They didn't mind it was a bit soggy and ate it all up!

Next day she say let's start again. We weighed and mixed everything carefully. Mum was very happy because she was listening to some music and humming the tune of her favourite concerto that Brooks made. She did this while we cooked but it went wrong again even when we didn't have a power cut and mum say she couldn't waste any more butter and things. We must buy one from the supermarket and decorate it and put candles on it and maybe nobody would know it wasn't homemade. IT WOULD BE OUR SECRET.

On my birthday, everyone sang to me, and I made a speech, and someone said, What l.........ovely party food your mum is so generous. And I said she is. Do you know she gave TWO big birthday cakes to the BIRDS! Then everyone laughed and I remembered it should have been a secret but I forgot and mum she laughed too.

Listening to music always makes my mum happy. Sometimes we go to the Festival Hall together, and I dress up in my best clothes and we have a glass of wine in the interval and I like it because it's special. Best of all, my mum likes violins and she teaches me the tunes so I know them and then the music isn't difficult. I love my mum. She is my bestest friend and looks after me all the days and nights because my Dad he died a long time ago.

This Christmas we went to Finland and saw the cathedral that looks just like a big wedding cake in the snow and my mum listened to her Siblus (Sibelius) *and she say Heaven couldn't be nicer. I love my mum.*

Still think she was worth less than the utmost I could do for her?

Thoughts of how we would cope with the future, and worse, how *she* would cope were I to fall off my perch ahead of her, were never far away. I found myself buying health supplements to guard against the ageing process, and joining a water aerobics class to keep me supple enough to go on doing all that was needed to run two lives smoothly. I not only had someone to live for, but someone I needed to *stay* alive for.

Often over the next two years, I read the promises I had made to myself prior to her going away. Allowing for the ups and downs of settling in, I must remain positive and share her enthusiasm. To outsiders it may have been seen as too short a time in which a decision should have been made. That's because for them, days still only contained the normal number of hours, and a week not suddenly a lesson in surviving eternity. And it had been the small things that had tipped the balance as is so often the case in life, but small things to which were not attributed importance.

We had been shaken by the experience and nothing would ever quite be the same again because each knew how near the precipice of loss we had walked. Always since her father's death, Minty's first words on waking had been, 'You won't die will you?' But now, as I crept in to open her curtains, they had changed to 'I like you and me. We'll live here for a hundred years and have nice days together. Always.' She was reminding me that life was good; each day too precious to squander in fear.

She had abandoned the dying thing, the prime anxiety for both of us of my going first. In that respect, whilst I remained locked in, she had moved on and I was encouraged. There was a distinct change of emphasis because we had gone through a rigorous training course on how to value the present. So in a strange way the parting had evoked a more positive attitude, a determination to value the day for its own sake and not to use it merely as a means of planning a safe end.

Without the articulation to express it, she had decided on a gamble. And her total surrender to my care drew us even closer. The fear that I might not outlive her would never pound less harshly for each passing year was a step nearer to the inevitable, but I must not shorten the span unnecessarily by debilitating anxiety.

Despite the likelihood of premature ageing, I had only feared illness for her as something that would make her suffer, but I never really addressed the graver possibility of her dying. Although time is a constant reminder that life rarely goes to plan, we are conditioned to think that we shall die in neat chronological order, generation by generation.

CHAPTER SIXTEEN

Not surprisingly, the assurance that transport would continue from home, had to be 'reviewed'. In short, by changing addresses, she had lost her place on the mini-bus, or rather on a list at Central Office. Each day, the bus continued to pass the house, and whenever I caught a glimpse of it there were empty seats, though of course I had no proof they wouldn't be filled before it reached its destination by 'new' handicapped people who had come to live in the area in the months Minty had been at Greenlands.

A fresh application must be made, and the process of form filling, the perusal of those forms by relevant departments, and the consideration of finance, was elongated to fill the next year. I was now the full time taxi driver and many times as I sat in traffic jams, or read outside a venue at which Minty was only required for a couple of hours, I imagined clerical personnel rubbing their hands in glee at the months they had stemmed the outflow from individual departmental budgets.

No use complaining for wasn't it a self-inflicted wound as far as Social Services were concerned - or was that my guilt? They had offered me the opportunity to enjoy a less exacting life, and I had brought her home again.

I couldn't deny the wear and tear. Inordinately tired one day after returning home from a thirty mile round trip before lunch only to be in a town equally distant in the opposite direction immediately afterwards, I realised I had lost a ring I'd worn for years. It was bitterly cold as I waited in the car park of the college whilst Minty was having a drama lesson and when she reappeared we eagerly anticipated a warm house and welcome cup of tea.

I had backed the same car into the same garage for the past seven years; why today did I catch the edge of the wing mirror in such a way as to tear it from its fixture? But I did, and we looked horrified at the splinters of glass that now lay strewn on the garage floor. Minty was there in an instant with pan and brush, reminding me there was nothing that could be done before tomorrow. Fingers numb we put the key in the door, I knew immediately that the heating system had failed. The house was like a morgue.

A smashed wing mirror, the loss of a favourite ring, and now a cold house with all the expense that such a situation might herald. I suddenly felt the aloneness of advancing years, and sat wretchedly on the kitchen chair wanting to scream my frustration. But as any parent of a handicapped person would understand, such profligate action was forbidden because of the distress it would undoubtedly cause. Feeling safe and secure depended on the equilibrium of your carer, so I said as calmly as I could, "Sweetie, I don't think I can take any more today. Let's get the kettle on and have a cup of tea before we try to sort things out."

I was so darned tired I hardly knew which end I was standing on. What a luxury it would be to be *told* what I had to do next.

Her tone was not censorious, only caring as she enveloped me in one of her bear hugs. "It'll be all right mum." And then she held my face in her two hands, smiled and comforted, "All those bad things in one day, but you've still got me!"

Trust my girl to shuffle priorities back into order. Such basic wisdom without the benefit of intellect. A tentative smile broadened as she convinced herself she was taking control.

"Absolutely right," I declared with a positivity I was far from feeling. "Come on. Let's go and light a huge fire in the lounge and toast our toes."

And from the grin that met the suggestion anyone would think I had prescribed Heaven itself. She was, I decided, the Almighty's justification for inventing the human race. I put a match to the fire and meanwhile my little companion had poured steaming tea into two identical mugs.

"Just what we need," I enthused. "Which is which?"

"Yours is the one with the sugar in it," she replied seriously, as if fearing I had lost my wits.

"Of course. Silly me." I waited for her to take which ever was the unsweetened one, and saw with amusement she had forgotten which way round they were.

As we sat by the flames now leaping in the grate, she looked at me seriously, put her cup down and said earnestly, "I want to tell you something in absolute confidence."

I knew immediately this was a phrase she would have heard on one of her soaps, and eager to know what interpretation she had placed on 'confidence,' I gave her my full attention.

She allowed a silence to fall, for all the world like the chairman of a company about to announce redundancies.

"I think you ought to sit down," she said gravely. "That's what people do when someone tells them something important."

"I am sitting."

"No, proper sitting - on a best chair."

"Right, let's go into the dining room."

The atmosphere was such that I almost started to believe a significant announcement was to follow. She brought two saucers and placed them under the mugs, obviously to give the announcement the dignity it merited.

"Are you ready?" she asked, and I nodded.

"Well this is it." She adjusted her sweater sleeve, and fixed me with her expression. Long pause, and then, "I want you to know you're the best Mum I've got!"

I waited deferentially to ascertain I wasn't interrupting further dialogue. "Then I'm very honoured. Thank you."

"That's alright. Was that a good announcement? How's your tea?"

The signature tune for 'Neighbours' could be heard and she was off, leaving me with the distinct impression I could expect promotion any day now!

Preparing the vegetables later for our evening meal, I realised we were short of milk and in the turmoil of the day had forgotten to stop by the convenience store.

"You be alright while I fly down to the shop?" I called to her.

"'Course I will. I'm an adult. You mustn't worry about me."
But getting out of the shop was a slower process than finding what I needed and I was a little longer than intended. As I approached the porch I saw a large handwritten notice in the window:-

'Dear Mum. I love you best. I put key under the mat. I go for nap now.'

"Welcome all burglars," I murmured. That would indeed have been the final straw today!

I thought long and hard that night. The solution was to simplify life; discard anything that was extraneous and time consuming for we were both anchored to her enforced childhood. In late sixties I was, in effect, still doing the school run; remembering the packed lunch and the outing money; preparing and repairing, constantly looking at my watch so as to be ready to collect on time, be at the next clinic appointment. ....Fine, just as long as I could stay healthy and active.

All my concentration must now be geared to that objective. Perhaps I should get some help with the garden. No point spending a whole morning fighting with deep-seated roots when a fit male could do this in half an hour. We had so far kept spare cash to pay for jobs we absolutely could not do; maybe the time had come to extend expenditure to jobs that took so much time and physical effort they threatened health and well-being.

It was a resolution that must wait for one more day, for tomorrow Minty had invited a friend. He would arrive before eleven, and be collected at six. i.e. early lunch, evening meal, and home in time for the soaps! Their timing was both judicious and predictable, and I love their total honesty. Why complicate a straightforward approach by variables? We had coffee together and I asked if they would like me to make soup and sandwiches at home, or go to the pub. No hesitation as both chorused, "Pub please."

Baguettes were an instant success as was the invitation by some of the locals to have a game of darts. They were pronounced undoubted winners, and on the way home Steven told me he had

168

'really enjoyed his lunch, and would choose it again next time he came!'

We played dominoes, and slow motion 'Snap', and then made some cakes together. Our visitor loved his cooking and turned out a batch of cakes worthy of taking to the tiny group with whom he now shared a home. Some basic detective work had indicated that apple pie was his favourite, and I thought fresh cream would finish off the evening meal nicely.

"Do you like cream with your apple pie, Steven?" I asked.
Again no preamble or polite 'just a little please.' I had asked a simple question and he would give me a candid reply.

"I prefer custard please," he said. "And I enjoyed coming."
This I knew was my cue to invite him to come again.

He hadn't quite finished his coffee when I saw him glance at his watch exactly as Minty would have done. It was precisely five fifty nine!

"I'll get my coat to be ready."

"I'll get your coat," I said. "You finish your coffee. Mr. Mills can have one too when he comes, if you'd like him to." But six was the appointed time; one minute past would be late and cause for concern. Fingers trembled a little and the worry more pronounced as his digital watch indicated 6.05. And then as a car pulled into the drive the smile returned. All was now according to plan. He drained his coffee and had a foot out of the door as his carer prepared to knock.

"Bye," he called. "I'm going to watch Emmerdale now!"

"Sorry about your coffee...." I called after them.

"I know my cue!" Mr. Mills called back. And I *was* five minutes late!"

* * *

In between my twenty mile round trips to the Centre and College in the neighbouring town, twice each day on three days a week, and a longer one to the Day Nursery on the fourth, the bid to regain transport continued.

We wouldn't only simplify our lifestyle, I decided. We must keep abreast of developments and ideas, and use them to Minty's

169

advantage. I had heard of a new initiative that may turn out to be yet another bandwagon, or, with luck have some genuine merit. I made the appropriate phone call, and yes, someone would call.

We were accustomed now to visitors bearing laptops and mobile phones, and again I was intrigued by the mass of information that went into them yet still failed to be communicated. Such information would be *accessible,* I was assured. But if it was, and yet remained untapped, surely that would identify a weakness within the system? The appointment of co-ordinator could make such a difference to the service overall. I spent so many hours on the road it was often difficult to establish contact and frequently the intended recipient of my calls was out of the office, and a message left on an answerphone resulted in another response left on mine.

"Sounds as if somebody in transport needs a call," the visitor said, and promptly attended to it. He was persuasive, and most importantly, he was effective. Whether an agreement was imminent and he gave the final turn to the screw, or had influence in the department I don't know, but transport on two, (maybe even three!) days, would be agreed as from the autumn. I was impressed, and imagined him going far, but then immediately decided that with such a natural and derisory inclination to cut through red tape, promotion might prove elusive.

Whilst I made coffee, he looked about him unselfconsciously. "Ever thought of selling your house and buying two flats in the same block?"

I confessed the notion hadn't crossed my mind, nor did I find it exactly tempting. With the need to be on site for my girl, I had made the garden my hobby and over the years it had become one that I loved and was in no hurry to offload.

"You could live in one and Minty independently in the other with as much outside care as she needed. That way, if anything happened to you she wouldn't be uprooted, and her care package would be established. It's an alternative to what you've just tried."

It all sounded very sensible, if not appealing. Was I selfish in not wanting to confine myself to an apartment block? And who would decide on the level of care? And could such care could be guaranteed to be ongoing when council belts were forever being tightened? And hadn't I leaned that questions like that didn't get answers in the modern system?

To date, perhaps because of all the publicity, I hadn't been overly impressed by 'Care in the Community.' I tossed the idea around. If she was entitled to a care package, why couldn't it be in her present home? I suppose the simple answer was that she was already here, and so was I. But it was an idea worth pursuing given that I might not always be able to drive or remain as active. A shift of emphasis in his suggestion would also ensure that whatever care was agreed, - and I had no illusions about the probable time scale involved, if indeed any could be arranged - would mean that the package could continue after my demise.

Was that the best plan, or should I be looking at another residential home. Where would she be best placed? And would anything stay reliably the same? That, I told myself was as naive as asking if political parties would always keep their promises. Any parent of a handicapped person will tell that gaining residence doesn't bring an end to anxiety. Homes close, staff and methods change and systems are upturned. So often I've heard parents of a physically handicapped young man declare that if 'Health and Safety' and its ever increasingly stringent rules were mentioned once more, they wouldn't be responsible for their actions.

"We hear more about what they *can't* do, than what they can," they sigh after the latest 'risk assessment.' "You begin to wonder who's doing the caring!"

On one of the days we drove to the Centre, the system decreed that once there, she would then be driven half way home again to where she would do some simple cooking and sandwich preparation for people wanting to hire rooms for conferences. As this venue lay midway between home and the Centre, it was at last agreed - after negotiations more suited to an international summit - that I should drive directly there. She would meet with her peers arriving by minibus from the Centre at the same time. Thus this became my 'lazy day' and one I anticipated gratefully.

Not only was the journey less time consuming, but she enjoyed her day there so much we asked if she could attend more often. The person in charge of the cooking programme seemed pleased at the prospect and it was agreed that one day could be increased to three. And in summer just as life became so much easier with time and mileage halved, it was agreed that Social Services would supply three days transport as from September!

With the prospect of a less demanding life ahead, the interim few weeks of to-ing and fro-ing to town didn't seem nearly so exhausting for there was now light at the end of the tunnel. Collecting her one afternoon, I noticed she was clutching a letter.

"Message for me?"

"Yes. It's to tell you that Mrs. Thomson is having an *eternity leaf*. We're going to get her a present."

An eternity ring, assuming Minty had misheard, seemed an unusual gift for anyone but a partner to give.

"She'll be very pleased with that," I said tentatively.

"No she won't. It's so heavy it makes her tired."

I was clearly not on the same wavelength. "What's an eternity leaf?"

"Silly old Mum," she laughed. "You know."

"No. My head won't tell me," I admitted. "You'll have to help me."

She grinned, exhaling as if wondering how to penetrate my failing brain. "It's when you're going to have a *baby!*"

"Oh, maternity leave," I laughed.

"That's what I told you!"

And I supposed that the long wait for an infant *can* seem like an eternity!

"And poor Mrs. Thomson can't play tennis anymore, so she says she'll have to be the vampire instead."

I fished for the car keys, my head filled with visions of a vampire wearing an eternity leaf!

* * *

Occasionally I am reminded that beneath her socially adjusted exterior is a much less competent intellectual skill. One of the hospitals we visited on a regular basis was part of a rebuilding programme and consequently the car-park was undulating and uneven and seemed to be littered with short stumps marking temporary parking spaces. Never adept at reversing, I urged Minty to hop out and watch them.

I wound down the window. "I'm not going to hit one, am I?"

"No."

Cautiously I reversed further. "Still good?"

"Yes fine. You're not hitting anything."

I eased back a few more inches and winced as I felt a soft 'thud' on the bumper.

"Oops! Now you are! I did watch them for you!"

* * *

The weekends were bliss, and provided a chance to work on a garden that was fast getting out of control. I was happily anticipating just such a couple of hours one Saturday when she called to me from the bathroom. "I'm going to make a special breakfast for us."

Her idea of 'special' means a pretty tablecloth, silver, the best china and table napkins.

"Why not! We'll have a lazy dressing-gown breakfast and then that hedge insists that I tackle it!"

It took some time as she meticulously placed everything on the table. The addition of a tiny vase of flowers did not surprise me, but I raised an eyebrow when a silver candlestick appeared. Undeterred she filled two bowls with generous helpings of cornflakes and handing me a box of matches, invited me to sit down and settled a newly laundered napkin on my lap.

"We might have a problem actually seeing the flame, Minty, with all this sunshine streaming in. Candles are usually meant for the evening."

She looked at me quizzically, paused for an idea to take shape, then instructed, "Wait," and plodded off to her bedroom. Minutes later the slow, ponderous footsteps could be heard retracing her steps. With an expression on her face suggesting polite toleration of my inability to engage any degree of imagination, a pair of

173

sunglasses was thrust earnestly into my hands. "Put those on. *Now* you'll be able to see the flame," she insisted.

By the time the table was fit to be deemed 'Savoy class', it was already almost nine, and I had visions of first the milkman, then the postman looking askance through the window at an elderly woman in a dressing gown, wearing sunglasses, and eating cornflakes by candlelight on a bright summer morning.

"There. Wasn't that special?" she asked, swallowing the last mouthful.

The candle was bending precariously under the fierce glare of the sun. How could such a morning *not* be special. Who needed a politician to think the unthinkable!

Dishes taken one by one to the sink, she invited me to go and see her exhibition of paintings. "Do you think you'll finish the hedge by eleven o'clock? That's when my exhibition will be ready. I've only got three more pictures to fix on my wardrobe," she said, "but I'm running out of blue-tac."

Having noticed the oxo size lump at the corner of each of her masterpieces when passing her bedroom, I wasn't surprised. In fact I think the pictures fell down due the weight of the blue-tac rather than stayed up because of it.

"Want a hand?" I asked.

"Please, but you mustn't look 'til you come for the opening."

"I'll only squint then whilst I help you."

By the time all her drawings were fixed she looked disconsolately at the one space remaining. "I haven't got time to do another picture before eleven."

"Why not have the exhibition this afternoon then?"

"No. I put a notice up to say it opens this morning."

There was only me to see the notice, but I knew better than to change the agenda. 'Set in stone' could have been invented for my daughter.

"I know," she said suddenly. "I'll use one out of that big calendar you gave me. It will fit exactly."

She pulled last year's 'Impressionist Paintings' calendar from her drawer and I wondered how Monet would have reacted to the idea of being used to fill a gap in an amateur exhibition!

Duly reappearing at the appointed time, there was a notice on her bedroom door. 'To come in - 10p for the hospice.' Not a bad price considering a welcoming glass of sherry was part of it!

"I know John has wine when we go to his exhibition," she said, "but I thought it was a bit early, so I'm doing sherry."

"Cooking or decent?" I teased.

"The one in the blue bottle with the black label - off the drinks trolley," came the reply.

"Worth lingering over then."

I dropped the coin into the 'Bisto' tin and proceeded to buy several works of art. Payment for the actual pictures was to go to Coronation Street stars because they hadn't won the best soap award this year. And we wouldn't like them to starve would we?!

My purchases were carefully rolled and packaged, and I prepared to leave.

"Just a minute Mum. You haven't paid."

I pointed to the tin. "It's in there."

"That was your coming in money. Now it's one pound to go out."

Unable to add up, and with absolutely no sense of the value of money, she'd nevertheless make a darned good businesswoman!

CHAPTER SEVENTEEN

A buxom, gregarious lady hooted at the gate on the first morning of my partial-retirement from the taxi run. She leapt out of the mini bus to see Minty on safely, checked that the seat belt was secure, then with an 'All Aboard!' they were on their way again. For all of her passengers she made the daily journey nothing less than an event. They sang, they joked, and they thought the world of her. With no formal training, only an innate bonhomie, she enervated, teased, and made the drive to town something they eagerly anticipated.

A highly competent driver, she was both practical and resourceful and worth her not inconsiderable weight in gold. Those who did gardening or cooking were dropped off with Minty, and those remaining continued to the Centre. A veritable Mrs. Santa Claus, each received cards and gifts from her. She was the highlight of their day and they adored her.

And life for me had resumed a manageable pace at last. We might even have time to sit with a holiday brochure soon. But I relaxed prematurely. Next morning's post presented a letter whose polite overtone veiled a hurt annoyance that my daughter had left the Centre after over twenty years without so much as a courtesy note to inform the authorities. But she was attending the same satellite, as I thought, to which Centre staff had previously taken her.

The only difference was that she now attended for three days, rather than one, and was being dropped off en route to avoid turning round and immediately retracing her journey. She was sharing the same programme and the same college course with the same friends who, living on the opposite side of town, were still being driven to the unit from the Centre. The venue, the course, the participants were exactly as before. Never, after so many years would I have removed her without prior consultation with those in charge. And I didn't think I had. I thought they were working in tandem to provide a service to those in their care.

With the apparent advantage of 'inside knowledge' a young man confidently enlightened me that I was mistaken in my assumption that one was a satellite of the other. Oh no, they were quite independent organisations now. Often I think organisations are so fragmented, and more money spent on the individual structure and administration of separate initiatives that councils are in danger of losing sight of their reason to exist.

"But she was taken to it *by* the Centre," I persisted. "I'm merely trying to prevent a lot of wasted time by going all the way into town only to be driven out again, especially as it has now been agreed for her to attend for three days each week."

And therein lay difference I was informed. Minty was *not* going into the Centre and then being driven out again. So she was not *registering* at the Centre.

"But couldn't registration be done at either place and communicated?" I asked. Evidently not. As he had said, they were independent of each other and managed completely separately. And was there anything else he could do to help?

I managed to chip in with a question before the phone could be replaced. "But why was she still considered to be at the Training Centre when *I* had done the driving and had asked if, to save time, petrol and frustration, I could drop her off at the unit which happened to be so much nearer to us. Why was it of no consequence that the unit was completely independent then?"

There was a pause. That must have been an arrangement to be helpful to me, he conceded, 'though slightly irregular.' Not wishing to cause awkward questions for those who had been helpful in 'a slightly irregular' way, I let the matter drop. The young man gained inspiration. "And of course, when you were doing the driving, your daughter was also remaining at the Centre for two days." He pressed his perceived advantage. "You do understand, don't you?"

177

I thanked him and apologised for my unintended discourtesy in failing to keep abreast of the dizzying rate of change in the system.

I'm sure there will have been reason behind his explanation. It was just beyond my intellectual power to divine it.

* * *

Councils often demonstrate an uncanny knack of not recognising an asset under their noses, but fortunately in this case, ours was correspondingly slow to realise an omission. A quiet mini bus pulled up at the gate one afternoon; no laughter, no smiles and a distinct absence of fun

A forlorn Sal helped Minty off and planted a kiss audibly on each cheek. "It's cheerio," she said, turning to me. "We've lost the contract. As of now. When I drop off the last one, I'm finished. Sorry, I don't know who's coming for her in the morning."

"But why...."

"Don't know. You'll have to ask the office."

It transpired that according to legal requirements Sal should not have been in sole charge of her passengers. Not difficult to see the sense behind the law in this case, but when her replacement was an uncommunicative driver, and assistant who appeared to be nodding off each time they arrived, I couldn't refrain from thinking that my daughter would be much safer in the hands of the competent, quick thinking Sal should an emergency occur. She would have lampooned a passer-by rather than let her charges be in any danger.

No matter that one so resourceful could be better than two who were less so, the law must be seen to be fulfilled, and the risk of litigation avoided. No room for individual consideration: those days had long gone. It was as if the magic had been switched off in the minibus. The little group was silent again; their faces bland, passive and unresponsive on the journey that now became routine and uneventful.

* * *

And in all the tumult of change I was grateful that her 'nursery job' remained the constant, albeit for only two hours a week. It had been arranged by Linked Employment, a department

178

whose personnel had done much to follow through on the philosophy of helping handicapped people to gain access to work, albeit for a short time providing the essential link and contact with those whose lives they emulated. And most participants made a worthwhile contribution, taking pride in the simpler mundane jobs that were an irritation to others. It could not however be a one sided initiative and depended on an altruistic approach from organisations willing to sign up to the scheme.

As the ageing process took its course, Minty's job description changed from classroom assistant to the grandiose 'P.A.' A morning with two year olds had gradually proved too demanding and I had expected the Principals, compassionate though they were, to withdraw their offer, but by now they had become fond of her and an alternative job in the tiny office miraculously 'became available.'

"I'm to help Mrs Mann in the office. It will be a very responsible job you know. I shall shred really important papers and tidy and photocopy and get the coffee. I shall be....." And here there was a pause as she endeavoured to recall, and pronounce, the word her employer had used. "Like jewels and diamonds," she struggled.

"Invaluable?" I offered.

"Yes. That's what I'm going to be! A PA-valable."

As the job has continued so the relationship has strengthened. On her birthday she receives flowers and cards from the children as any other member of staff, and at Christmas is thoroughly indulged. It is a very special place and to the credit of its Principals she continues to feel genuinely needed. I'm not sure just how 'valable' her work is to the essential running of the nursery but who can tell how many attitudes have been affected over the years by the interaction she has with staff, children, parents, workmen, and delivery men.

Arriving to collect her one lunchtime, I braked at the entrance to allow the postman to pull out. He lowered the window of his van, grinned and said, "You must be Mum? She's really nice." Never having had contact with Downs before, he took pleasure in admitting his surprise at how much he had enjoyed the chat he had had with her, and indeed the fact she was capable of any communication at all.

She was fairly buzzing with excitement as she got into the car. "Mum, you do realise I work for a *very important organisation* don't you?"

"Of course! One of the best."

"And do you know how you can *tell* it's important?"

With its demountables and low, timber classrooms it could hardly be called an aesthetic or impressive building. The car park was pot-holed and council storage sheds framed its perimeter, so I said merely, "Go on. You tell me."

There was a heady intake of breath, and she said with a pause between each word, "It has the biggest...birthday ...banner... I... have... ever ...seen!"

"Wow! And did it come out for you today?"

"Yes. And everyone sang to me."

So ICI, Rothschilds, Barings, forget your position on the FTSE, the dividend you declared to your shareholders, your trading price on the stock market, and your profit margins. Just make sure your staff birthday banner remains competitive!

But frustrations exist in the 'bestest workplaces.' The nursery in common with many schools and colleges, couldn't provide all the equipment and learning aids it would ideally like to offer and staff had been delighted when the council had set up a toy-loan scheme; tough, good quality toys to benefit large numbers of children in turn. Not long after it was initiated, the Principal phoned for a particular piece to be delivered, only to be told that the scheme was no longer functioning because 'the person who had run it had left'.

No matter, she would go and collect her request. But the toys had been 'put away somewhere' and no one knew where to find them. And so another enterprise had been launched - the idea might possibly have been instrumental in a career move for an aspiring individual, and expense would certainly have been incurred in the purchase of sufficient toys to make the scheme viable - and now with so many other ideas, it lay dead in the water.

Does one have to be a cynical outsider to feel that sometimes the word 'progress' has developed another connotation, and now means 'progression from one idea to another without actually making an advance'?

CHAPTER EIGHTEEN

With her weekly two hours at the Day Nursery, and culinary work at the cooperative (the initiative that wasn't a satellite), Minty was fully occupied and happy. Staff came from the College she had previously attended to run successive courses, so with three days of planned activity for her, I too felt the strain being eased.

Unaware of the amount of study, commitment and cerebral activity required, I joined a Bridge class. I made little headway but it was as promised, a social game, and through it I increased my circle of friends. Whatever has been forgotten from our Klinger textbooks, none of the group who came to my house for our 'practice mornings' will forget the day we were all engrossed by the dealer's audacious bid for a slam and the concentration involved to achieve it. At a crucial moment in the silence, the phone rang and Minty whose session had been cancelled that morning, lifted the receiver and was heard to say, "I'm sorry. My mother can't come to the phone just now. She's tied up with three men!"   She forgot to ask who was calling so I was unable to explain.

Dizzy with unaccustomed free hours, I also enrolled with a reading group now that in theory, on three days of the week I needed only to be back at base by four o'clock. Of course numerous phone calls, meetings, referrals, assessments of the 'current situation', and long hours in hospital waiting rooms as there are for all carers of handicapped people, ate into much of this 'free time.' Dental appointments and the like were arranged around her programme, but nevertheless the frantic driving schedule had eased.

Maybe it *was* time to take a holiday; to put some distance between us and the abortive attempt to live separate lives.

Holidays are probably the most difficult time in that it isn't easy to juxtapose two lives in a setting other than the familiar. And Minty's eyesight is so poor that she only has a vague impression of scenery that for me is an essential ingredient of any trip. She picks up on atmosphere, is fascinated by unfamiliar cuisines, climates and customs, but misses her television, and always looks forward to talking about her soaps to anyone who hints at a similar enthusiasm for them.

But now we had a new problem. Whereas in the past she had happily stayed with her godparents whilst I took an occasional long haul trip, I could tell that she was now only keen to do so as long as I was 'at base.' I knew that she feared, as I did, another '9/11', which might prevent me coming back to her. If we were together and it happened, then that was fate. Whether totally due potential disaster, or still the effects of living away from home was difficult to assess. I couldn't put it all together in my mind yet, hence we planned a trip to the Greek Islands where I hoped there would be enough for both to enjoy.

The journey to the airport was uneventful. There were no delays and we settled to enjoy the flight. Only Minty could have sent her *'cobliments to the chef'* after a package airline meal, but an amused stewardess responded appropriately.

I suggested we went to freshen up before a queue formed. Ever compliant, she eased herself into the aisle, moved a few steps and then quite suddenly was overcome by severe spasms. Her pulse was haywire, and though cold and clammy she complained of the heat. Another passenger helped me to support her and set her down on a cabin-crew seat.

"Water. Quick!" I instructed a young steward. The moment was desperate and it was not until long afterwards when we were on an even keel again that we were able to laugh at his reaction.

"Sparkling or still Madam?" he had asked feebly.
I grabbed a bottle from his trolley. Still unable to free himself from his obvious recent training, he ignored my apparent rudeness and said mechanically, "That will be one euro please."

She shook for what seemed an eternity and became so weak that the flight staff radioed for paramedic assistance to await our arrival. The prospect of being ferried to the nearest hospital with no Greek at my disposal and only enough medication for the holiday period made my pulse quicken. If only we were on our return journey...

She slept for two days, taking only sips of water as I sat beside her, and then gradually and miraculously it became almost impossible to tell that anything had been wrong. She dressed for dinner, watched a demonstration of Greek dancing, and beamed with sheer pleasure when invited to join in. She followed instructions to the letter but as with anything requiring mental activity, her reactions were slow. When everyone else gracefully stepped to the right, Minty threw them all by moving to the left. Chaos reigned as our holiday companions fell about in hysterics. Waiters appeared with 'Ozo' and precipitately a party was in full swing.

It did however shorten the period for which we are normally given a wide berth on holidays. People unacquainted with handicap don't know what to expect. Shy or embarrassed, they stay on the periphery, avoiding direct involvement in case she might 'throw a wobbly' or behave unsociably. By the fifth or sixth day, when her demeanour has remained constant, some make friendly overtures, use her name and greet her cheerfully.

By the penultimate day, invariably fellow guests are asking for her address so that they can keep in touch! And they do. She continues to receive gifts on her birthday from three couples we met as long as ten years ago.

* * *

Once home, I discussed the occurrence with our doctor, though with the patient appearing to be in rude health, my report could hardly sound less convincing. However, he guessed what I was thinking and didn't resort to platitudes.

"You're concerned it was a mini heart attack." He looked down at the desk and then met my eyes again. "She seems robust now but as the years go by we need to be prepared for sudden deterioration."

I appreciated his inference that I was not alone in caring for her.

"And of course she can stay on a plateau for a long time," he added.

"You mean it isn't axiomatic I shall predecease her?"

"You know I can't answer that. But I think you should set aside this constant fear you're going to leave her behind."

The gently expressed sentiment carried an understanding tone but our acquaintance was too long-standing for further words to be needed.

I knew the folly of wanting a crystal ball, but at least I'd be able to plan and be prepared. Most essentially I want to outlive her and be around to care for her to the end, but life doesn't always give us what we think is best. And could I be certain I'd cope with one outcome better than the other?

I would gamble that there isn't a day goes by when older carers up and down the country don't think about the problem, and yearn for a better system than now exists. A system that if only governments with perspective would genuinely look at needs, could save them millions in finance, and carers a commensurate amount in heartache. Yes it would need some fine-tuning, imagination, and commitment across political party boundaries, but it *could* work. And it would have to be done nationally.

Many of us with offspring who did nothing to deserve being born handicapped, would wish to care for them at home within the family. But we would like to be linked to the type of care home of our choice *in case* of need; to be able to make regular visits and become familiar with the layout and the way things are done – much the same as visiting cousins or friends. We would offer voluntary help there, as we did along with many others who had been affected, to the hospice in which my husband had died. Indeed much could be learned from the Hospice Movement.

If the parent outlived the handicapped person and remained fit enough to care, and happy to do so, there would be no call on government expense. If on the other hand need did arise, the handicapped person would be moving to a place and people who were familiar. No panic measures to get a place in case we die, or angst that our handicapped sons and daughters will be slotted anywhere a place can be found.

Yes, one can of course see the problems, but they are not insuperable. It needs joined up thinking, and cooperation between agencies all linked to a central 'nerve centre' that recognises its least able citizens as more than statistics.

Some of us with less severely handicapped sons and daughters have tossed the idea of both parent and offspring going into the same residential care home when the ageing process refuses any longer to be denied, and for whichever one remaining to continue warden-assisted residency. It would surely cost no more, and probably a great deal less, than current 'solutions.'

***

Like all new initiatives the cooperative became ripe for some cost cutting, and the inevitable phone call came.

"I'm sorry I know how much they hate change," the lady who had done simple cookery with the group said. "The fact is I'm not to have my contract renewed."

Once again no sooner had we established a routine of doing something worthwhile than the goal posts were to be moved.

"But who'll come in your place?"

"No one. The unit is to be managed by the other two members of staff."

I was perplexed. The other two people were both superb, both valued by the group, but male and both gardeners."

"Won't that get a bit confusing?"

Apparently one was to be put in charge of overall catering for when groups hired rooms for meetings, and I assumed to drum up business so that the venture could be self-supporting. Minty and her friends would help to make sandwiches and coffee for such occasions and serve them at appropriate times. If someone had to be offloaded, it must be the one on temporary contract, irrespective of gender or skills offered.

The disappearance of one third of the staff caused the expected reaction and confusion. Leaving their instruction room and kitchen, the tiny group moved to the larger house on the same site. Not only were two staff to do what three did previously, but must also manage a larger area, generate 'business' with all the associated administrative processes, and yet still be accessible to their charges who tried to cope with their individual problems and anxieties in the unfamiliar and confusing situation.

And one instructor, whilst no doubt thankful he still had a job, was being asked to tackle a subject that was outside his remit, with the predictable difficulties. But the books had been balanced. What could be more important?

If I were to name any one thing that was problematic across the spectrum of handicapped people, I would put 'Change' at the top of the list. Any change demands significant time for adjustment. Overnight, knee-jerk reactions to cutbacks are nightmares for them to cope with. And some don't.

Those involved were less confident due the absence of a familiar figure waiting for them in the same place each morning, with ideas about what to make for lunch, which cakes to bake for visitors etc, and the days were consequently less creative and inspiring as everyone adjusted to new demands and circumstances.

Questions to the authorities met with seemingly rehearsed jargon. The base must be viewed not as a training centre but a place where the handicapped could prepare for work. It was a mystery to me that to prepare people for work, training is reduced and the staff less accessible to those who need them most, because, as a result of reductions and wider job descriptions, they are expected to be in several places and don numerous hats at the same time.

Not long after, the College too, presumably also for financial reasons, was unable to continue to send someone to run courses - or rather two people to run them. One was more than capable of coping with the tiny group involved, but 'Health and Safety' deemed she must have an assistant even though other trained adults were on site. And as two were obviously a greater drain on the budget, the expense was unsustainable.

Thus another enthusiastic period was short lived. For older carers, the letters and phone calls for which we had energy and zeal as young parents, become wearing because experience has alerted us to the futility of attempts. But our offspring are the Peter Pans of this world and try we must. Finally, when it becomes evident that however exhausted, we shall not 'go away,' it is usually agreed that a meeting 'will be arranged.'

The phrase reminds me of the initial consultation at a hospital. The condition is not treated or cured but the patient has been seen, and within a necessary time to meet political targets. When there's a problem, let's have a meeting about it. That way it will be recorded that 'something has been done' and action has been taken.

For nearly two hours, two senior personnel from the authority (I wondered why one would not have done,) in addition to one of the staff members now left, i.e. fifty per cent, talked over the particular concerns that my daughter and I expressed. It was made clear to me that as a result of this time given to her, similar meetings would now have to be offered to each of the other trainees, now called members, the term 'clients' having also been discarded. The experience of advancing years however makes one wonder how many such consultation meetings actually did take place.

I watched the scenario, mentally calculating the cost of professional time and travel expenses of fifteen such meetings - assuming the gardening group would be treated similarly. Set against the cost of retaining a temporary member of staff, would much of a financial advantage really have been gained? But of course 'dealing with concerns' might have been financed from another pot. 'As long as it can come out of a nest other than the one I'm sitting on ......'

All very familiar from my last years in teaching. No question of being able to transfer money from one pot that didn't need it to augment another that did in order to achieve a worthwhile state overall. Nothing so sensible. Just find a way to spend it for the purpose allocated, or it would be viewed as not being needed, and consequently deducted from next year's budget. I expect that's why there is such activity on road repairs just as the financial year is to run out.

CHAPTER NINETEEN

Despite the teething problems, two staff members found themselves covering for what three previously accomplished, trying to generate take-up of the services offered, keeping the premises attractive to would be clients, and ensuring their charges were occupied. It was an unrealistic expectation, and not surprisingly that vital human contact on which so many mentally handicapped rely for motivation, suffered.

To avoid the inactivity I had already expressed concern about, it was agreed that Minty could help now and then in the office. I could always tell from the way she walked down the drive whether or not the day had been interesting. Returning home particularly jauntily on one occasion, she proudly announced she had done her boss' accounts. She possesses virtually no numerical skill and I was intrigued.

"Really?"

"Yes. There was just a *little* problem. I couldn't see the figures!"

"That must have made it difficult," I said thinking that creative accountancy must have come into its own today. And then she looked so worried, and said, "I really did want to help him, but I couldn't see."

"Then its best to tell him. He'll understand."

"No. I couldn't hurt his feelings."

I knew we were in one of her emotional quagmires, and though drawing analogy after analogy, I made no headway. Finally I said, "If Chris asked me to run a mile in five minutes I would have to tell him that much as I would like to, I just couldn't. But I wouldn't be hurting his feelings."

I thought she had understood until she patted my hand and said, "Of course you wouldn't Mum, 'cos he knows you're old."

Letting people down, hurting feelings, not making dreams come true, are all the same side of the coin for her, and must be avoided at all costs. She understands only black and white; shades of grey are outside her comprehension. She answers questions honestly and comments frankly on situations as they appear to her.

Sadly the office arrangement couldn't continue because of the risk of accusation of abuse. Perfectly understandable from the male member's position, though had I had been given any cause for concern, I would not have allowed her to continue to attend after the departure of the female member of staff. Others understandably felt very strongly that there should be a female on site, and attendance by their offspring ceased.

It is difficult not to suspect that diminishing attendance would be welcome to councils. Non-provision of services on the basis they are not required would then be justified, not to mention the money that would be saved. Some of the units are on very desirable sites and councils with shrinking budgets must be straining at the leash to accept offers from developers, whilst property with fields or gardens attached would be perfect locations for society weddings and high profile functions.

Familiar jargon was regurgitated. There were no such plans afoot. 'It was all about valuing people, using their skills, making them feel they mattered and had something to contribute.' Which was really code for cutbacks and a pruned budget. And when the rooms were hired and refreshments requested, there was indeed an air of business and being needed. On such days buffets were served and the 'members' (previously trainees, clients, service users,) were busy and radiated a sense of purpose.

One particular Friday had been brisk with three bookings to be catered for, and Minty who loves such activity and the contact that results, looked tired when she came in, but happily so.

"Good day?" I asked. "You look as if you've been busy."

"I have. It was hectic. Lots of people to look after."

"Wow, I hope you stopped long enough to have your own lunch."

"Yep. But not my lunchbox. I had a special *laxative* lunch with my boss."

"What!"

"I was very important. I was staff today, and we had a lot of pressure to get everything ready on time, so Chris he say we'll suffer from laxative stress if we aren't careful!"

Imagination went into overdrive. I had visions of high-powered executives up and down the country, scrunched expressions contorting their faces as they queued for every available office loo!

"I'll have to remember I live with an executive now! But it was a lot of fun too, wasn't it?"

"It was." She looked wistful. "You know I really like my boss."

Unintentionally I had set her on a path we had travelled many times in the past. This longing for a mate, for someone special; in fact the normality that others take for granted, is so often denied to the Downs community. They are reminded of it with every film, every 'soap', every human situation that confronts them, and their longing is as deep, their yearning as strong as any other member of the human race. This of course can put them in a highly vulnerable position. And a very lonely one.

I recalled how, soon after her father had died, and she still in her twenties with the normal feelings of any young woman, had pleaded with me to find someone for her - or even someone for both of us if that was the best I could manage! Explaining as gently as I could that complying with such a request was not quite like shopping for a box of biscuits, I tried to share some of the agony by pointing out that we were both alone and trying to be strong.

She saw my attempts as flimsy, obviously thinking there was a better solution than merely putting up with the situation.

"What would your favourite fellow look like?" she persisted.

We had been watching the Wendy Craig series of 'Butterflies' and I decided to describe Thomas, the unflappable chauffeur.

"So he will have a grey suit and green cap," she said thoughtfully, as if having identified the appearance of our non-existent housemate, we were half way there. "And what sort of a car will he drive?"

191

Renault Lagunas were few and far between on the English roads at that time so I plumped for that particular model and chose racing green as the colour. It was many months afterwards whilst clipping the hedge together that a car drew up and its driver asked directions to a location some three miles distant. He thanked me, wound up his window, and prepared to pull out into the road again. I could feel a tugging at my sweater, which was unusual for never had I known her to interrupt.

"Bye," the driver called cheerfully. "Thanks for your help!"
The tugging continued. "You let him go," she said disbelievingly. "And he was driving a green Renault Laguna!"

Now, so many years later, I poured her a cup of tea and we sat again for the chat that comforted for a while but never really compensated for that which could not be. She was hurting; I could feel her pain. And there was nothing in the world I could do about it. Over a lifetime, we had found at least partial solutions to her problems but in this I was powerless.

"You know that your boss is happily married sweetie, and he can never be more than a work friend."

She lowered her eyes and I thought she was struggling to accept the reality, brutal though it seemed, and her sudden unexpected, matter of fact reply rendered my platitudes meaningless.

"But I had a crush on him *before* he was married, when he used to work at my Centre, and he *still* didn't choose me."

Oh for a slice of political jargon to deal with this one!

Emotion switched off as rapidly as it had claimed her. "You forgot to put a fork for my coleslaw in my packed lunch."

"But you work in a kitchen. You could have borrowed one."

"Silly old Mum - on Fridays I'm staff! But it didn't matter 'cos I had my lunch with Chris."
Obviously run of the mill stainless steel that she used when cooking as a 'student' on Tuesdays and Wednesdays, wasn't good enough when suffering from laxative stress on Fridays!

192

I thought again that night about the irrepressible longing for a mate. In her twenties she had longed for the white dress, the limousine, the walk down the aisle and a normal physical relationship. Now as she had aged, it had calmed into just wanting someone close with whom to share the moments. A sure sign my Peter Pan was physically growing older.

CHAPTER TWENTY

The Americans were making distinct warlike noises and the invasion of Iraq seemed not only inevitable, but imminent. An old friend, an Iraqi we hadn't seen for some years had telephoned out of the blue and after exchanging an update of news, was invited for lunch the following Saturday. I suspected he needed assurance of long-standing friendships given the current volatile situation.

Just prior to leaving his house over an hour's drive away, he phoned apologetically. "This must be the time of year our stars have decided old friends should meet again," he said.

Two ex-lecturer colleagues with whom he had lost touch over the years had evidently located him and turned up unexpectedly. He didn't want to be inhospitable by leaving immediately to come to us, and in any case was delighted by their arrival. Could lunch be delayed awhile - he had insisted it was just a sandwich....so nothing to spoil?

"Why don't you all come," I said. "That way they can have more time with you and we shall have your company for longer."

Hearing this exchange Minty was already laying two extra places at the table. I turned down the oven and lowered the beef bourguignon to the bottom shelf.

"Are they ladies or men?" she asked.

I realised I hadn't asked. "Does it matter?"

"Yes. I give the men the big white napkins and the ladies lacy ones," she explained.

"Probably men. Better give us all big linen ones just in case."

We heard the car in the drive. Three Middle Eastern gentlemen eased themselves out and approached the house. Our friend greeted us warmly and introduced his companions, who, to my consternation were both carrying supermarket bags.

"A modest contribution to the lunch," said one, pulling out a large loaf. "Josef said we would be having English sandwich."
I glanced at our friend who, grinning conspiratorially, discreetly placed a bottle on the work surface knowing full well lunch would be otherwise.

"And something to accompany it," added the other, offering an additional bottle of merlot.
Relieving them of their coats, I whispered to Josef, "Could you repeat their names? Minty won't have caught them."

We went into the sitting room and he took her hand. "So my special one, come and say 'hello' to your visitors. This is my friend Ahmed and he is an Arab. And this gentleman is Modani and he is Palestinian. And you already know that I'm Josef, an Iraqi."
She held out her hand. "How do you do," she said seriously. Then assuming from the introductions that we all needed to *be* something, added, "I'm Mum's daughter, and I'm Downs."

The ice was well and truly broken, and the laughter and repartee that was to continue for several hours, erupted. Minty helped to ease dishes around the table, making sure that everything was to hand. And when everyone was replete she quietly transferred crockery to the kitchen.

"She's wonderful," Ahmed smiled. "So capable."
"I couldn't manage without her," I replied, knowing she could hear me and that such praise was manna to her.

And as the world waited for war to be declared, Arab, Jew, Muslim and Christian had sat together to share a meal. After the casserole and desert, I had returned the planned savoury biscuits to the cupboard, and with our cheese we drank wine, and broke bread from Tesco's.
And the poignancy of the moment escaped no one.

"That was nice," she said, after they'd gone. "That's what I missed when I was away."

And it couldn't be denied that despite her handicap, she had contributed to the most comfortable and rewarding of atmospheres, that of being with friends.

Reflecting later on the day's events, it came home to me that because of the way life had evolved, my response to Ahmed's compliment to her had perhaps not been far from describing the truth, for she gave meaning and purpose to my day. To change the status quo would be harder now than ever before and test us both to the hilt.

Yes I was tied, as friends seemed unable to stop reminding me, and increasingly so as daily activity options for her diminished. But she returns love, that most fundamental of human needs, in such vast quantities, that what had seemed such a catastrophe over forty years ago when, on that winter's night in Canada our doctor told us she was handicapped, had also proved to be an unimaginable blessing.

The impending war had put things into perspective. With all its failings, ours was not a bad country to be in. And compared with mothers in Iraq, my problems were miniscule.

CHAPTER TWENTY ONE

I have never been convinced by the 'prioritising' theory whereby some things are attributed less important status. Ignore them and they come back ten times the size. But this time, try as I might, I couldn't juggle all that needed to be fitted into one day. My daughter's 'job' and a clinic appointment I had awaited for months clashed irreconcilably. Perhaps I could ask if anyone was available from one of the many departments with which she is 'on file' to take her on the twenty minute drive to the Day Nursery. I would be free in time to collect her.

A thoroughly pleasant voice explained sympathetically that colleague A had left, colleague B was on long term sick leave, and manning the department alone, the owner of the voice could not possibly help. That all seemed entirely reasonable and I thanked her and was about to ring off. She could, however, give me a number of an organisation that would prove helpful. I was to let her know how I fared.

But the said organisation required notice, not because they had no one available, but because forms must be first completed and returned to them with the annual membership fee. Only then could registration take place. And I wondered why the driver couldn't have brought the forms and collected the fee on arrival. Over the years I've learned that simplicity is not a comfortable bedfellow for bureaucracy. The more complicated a situation can be made, the more paperwork generated, the more targets are met!

But the call had given me an idea. There was a community service in a small town a few miles away - a group of volunteers organised by someone I had known and respected from my teaching days.

And yes they would help. If I wished I could make a contribution towards petrol, and a very capable lady with experience of Downs would be with me in good time. She was indeed competent and professional, and won my daughter's heart immediately. She even phoned to tell me as soon as they arrived and that she would make sure Minty was happily installed before leaving. And if ever I was in need again, I mustn't hesitate to phone.

Efficient, dependable and compassionate. A voluntary organisation unimpeded by red tape. No form filling, no-fuss, just action at the moment of need.

It was some time later that the recipient of my earlier call rang to see how I'd got on. I explained about the necessity to fill in forms and that I had been able to make an alternative arrangement.

"Oh, but I could have got those for you."

I paused, thinking I must have misheard. "No, they needed to have them back signed, before I could use the service," I said.

"Yes but they're very simple. I could have brought them out and returned them to the organisation for you."

To do that would incur more than twice the mileage, more than twice the time as actually doing the short journey I had requested. And yes I could appreciate that once the forms were completed I could use the service again without bothering anyone, but it didn't change the fact that today she was without colleague A who had left and colleague B who was on long term sick leave.....

Cooperating with bureaucracy from where I and many other lifetime carers are standing, the process becomes wearying and demoralising. And all the time anno domini is kicking in leaving us increasingly unconvinced that endless paperwork does other than identify needs. Often, without realising the exact moment of decision, the carer resolves to conserve what energy is left for coping alone; finding his or her own solutions.

The council employee, the social worker in turn becomes less involved, aware that there are no brownie points for actually helping the focus of one's job. Greater the career prospects if you can come up with a new idea or initiative, something to put the relevant council on the map. If the various agencies appear to be lumped together in carers' minds, that is how they appear in the confusion generated by the 'Press 1 for this' 2 for that, 3 for all other enquiries' regime.

"She's on sick leave, holiday leave, at a meeting, on a course," we hear. We want her here with people who need help, and who will teach her the job better than any course. Real people with real problems, but who cannot articulate their own fears and anxieties.

It is now considered that half the nation can cope with a university education. Surely if the programmes provided are good enough and the students genuinely up to standard, they don't need to return for so many day courses so soon after qualifying?

'But of course staff need to be updated because legislation is constantly changing.'

And isn't that the nub of the problem? Our society is obsessed with change and the legislation it produces, and more than ever before, with covering backsides. If goal posts are moved, rules amended and numbers crunched often enough, people can be fooled into mistaking change for progress. Or can they?

Another course; another bit of worthless paper to indicate an extra 'qualification' so that competency can be assumed. Is there not a resulting danger that some at the top of the ladder will know less about the real world than those who have planted their feet firmly on the ground by honestly getting stuck in rather than talking about it? Involvement at the coalface, practical application, can teach more than any theory in a lecture hall.

For sanity's sake, let's go back to honest commitment, human interaction, and due regard for loyalty and experience.

Reformed, re-titled, reorganised, rescheduled, and finally prompted to resign. Stay around and promotion might be offered; with luck - because there's nobody else left to do the job, or on merit for filling in the right boxes and meeting targets imposed by governments only interested in reducing numbers and expense.

I imagine personnel who have been despatched to endless meetings (one can only imagine the cost,) to become acquainted with further change and directives, barely realise they too have been brain washed and in time regurgitate prepared statements in the way of politicians on the Today programme. They are so relieved to bring to mind an approved phrase that they don't realise their words are no longer plausible because the carer has heard them from so many mouths in so many forms so often before. Empty phrases fuelled by the empty heart of politics.

"Whatever do they find to talk about at all these meeting!" I heard one parent despair. "And does it do any good when they've *talked* about it! Why don't they talk to us instead?"

To the Carer looking in it seems so many Social Services personnel leave because the system doesn't allow them to get on with the job, and with their departure go parental hopes of ever getting more than a superficial sham of a service. Good social workers who choose to stay are spread so thinly that everybody wants them, until they too can only oversee a service in crisis and invariably take the flack for those less committed.   Maybe that's why my calls went unheeded at the most crucial time of Minty's residence.

I'm told that they fly and skim across an area so wide they collapse under the strain of mountains of directives, legislation and too many calls from too many bosses, none of whom seem able or willing to stand up and say to government that what is demanded is not feasible, for fear, I suspect, of being labelled a failing authority.

Forms are completed to prove contact with clients, but so often to no more effect than to leave them frustrated by the lack of follow up. On paper, criteria are met, 'excellence' striven for, but in reality the very people central to new initiatives are pushed further and further towards the periphery. Consequently there is less eagerness on the part of the handicapped to avail themselves of watered down provision, thereby playing into hands of those who would cut costs by closing places down 'because there is no longer a call for them.'

Friends with a severely and doubly handicapped son have had eleven social workers in three years. Many don't have one at all. Yes in law, a handicapped person must have one. But try and get a name from the authorities! If the situation is dire, one will be produced from the pot but when people with Downs are living so much longer, such a policy will surely only stack up problems for the future.

What is needed is a single supportive relationship, not a succession of people skating superficially across the surface of a life already made formidable by handicap itself, and making no impact other than to record statistics.

I have yet to meet a member of Social Services who is honestly happier with the work they are doing since the entry into their lives of targets, mission statements, league tables and mountains of bureaucracy, not to mention the jobs that have been created to manage them. It's not something they can express publicly, finding it better to keep their heads down and look forward to a pension.

I hear talk that soon residential homes may be a thing of the past for those not severely disabled. Of course the political stance for each change is that such individuals can live a more 'rewarding' life in the community. Rewarding for whom? Independent living is now the catchword. Not a lot of difference in concept from 'care in the community' except that that scheme didn't work; in fact led to some catastrophic developments. So it must be renamed, revamped and promoted as the ultimate brainchild.

There are advocates to promote it, umpteen schemes to 'enable' it (on paper if not in reality,) and a whole body of bureaucrats with eyes blinkered to prevent their seeing that however they dress it up some people, having been born handicapped, will remain handicapped; that very few of the *disabled* can, as a result of medication or acts of parliament, become *enabled*. Is it not part of the philosophy of any civilised society that the lucky ones care for our least able citizens?

Everything appears to be short term and money driven no matter how situations are angled to convince us otherwise. In any case, many of us have been around too long to be fooled any more by the PR presentations. Layers of management to oversee numerous costly changes and innovative ideas, often I feel, overlooking the fact that the community is unready or unwilling to receive them.

Elderly carers up and down the country are not blindly and selfishly clinging on; but yearning desperately for stability and cohesion in a state system that is all too variable. Painfully we come to accept that the safe future we try so desperately to plan has its foundations on the shifting sands of politics.

To my mind, the system has collapsed, and far from being rebuilt, a new generation has inherited the collapse and thought that *was* the job. They have massaged and stuck flags on it and to cope with the insecure, foundationless pile, they tiptoe precariously over it knowing that promotion will come through being willing to be part of the 'kidology' because on a personal level a mortgage has to be paid, and children put through university to satisfy another government target.

Some have stayed for job satisfaction. Their pay was not extraordinary but enabled a decent standard of living. Now with house prices needing monopoly money, people at all levels leap from what rightly or wrongly appears to be a sinking ship, to jobs offering greater income. It is facile to say money is a god, but property has become the demon.

I look at forms filled in by graduates - peppered with grammatical errors - that will be entered into the 'system.' It's evidently possible now to graduate without being able to put a coherent sentence together. And in today's absence of articulate speech, we have become a nation of jargon-spouters.

I wonder why I hadn't noticed such errors years ago, but in the past there wasn't the mound of paperwork to be compiled, distributed, then agreed by 'the client.' The focus was on demonstrating a practical ability to get things done. Not world shattering things, but often small changes that made the big difference to so many lives. It was more than enough that the midwife delivered my children safely into this world. Whether or not she had a good turn of phrase was immaterial. What was *done* was what created the impression, not reporting on a situation that 'requires attention,' as if that exonerates the author from actually attending to it.

I recalled many 'old pro's' in the nicest sense of the word, whose substantial information about their patients was in their heads, built up over the years because they stayed in the job and gained recognition for reliability and commitment. They wouldn't have been fooled by ticks in boxes. Safe and stable, the job was productive, effective and valued.

And just as Matrons disappeared from our hospitals, so the real person with whom the buck ends has gone from other national institutions. Someone who has a name; someone accessible who listens and acts, and takes responsibility. Such an invaluable character has been replaced by 'Mandy' 'Darren' 'Tracey,' the 'Have a nice day brigade' who leave at the end of a week for a job that pays better. No time for introspection or to look honestly at a situation and dwell on important issues. Must respond to x no of calls an hour, - superficially, flippantly, but reaching TARGETS. Whoopee!

"Oh that's not our department any more. It's dealt with by …..I'll give you a number."
Well, after a frustrating hour of trying to get someone to pick up the phone, that's some progress. Isn't it? An indifferent, disembodied voice can be heard. 'Sorry there's no one here to take your call…… '

Oh for a central system that coordinates and communicates efficiently, and with personnel who deal in human nature not number crunching.

I'm aware that the argument for recording is that information can be shared with other 'providers and agencies' – hence mobile phones, emails, laptops to facilitate slick communication, only to find that to cover backsides it's safer to send a copy to every Tom Dick and Harry. Like junk mail, copies appear to remain unopened, unread, and unimportant. No matter, the right boxes have been ticked and litigation avoided. More important to attend a succession of meetings with bulging briefcase and a new identity badge indicating the umpteenth job title, to become updated and informed, and no doubt frustrated.

And would we mind the 'cuts' and tightening of council belts if we didn't see such inordinate waste resulting from poor organisation and inefficient management?

The job has become a river; no longer a rock on sure foundation, and the only way to survive on water is to jettison all that can be discarded in order to stay afloat. Paddling through rapids takes all one's concentration, leaving none for the minutiae that constitute the whole. A frightening tsunami has replaced solid ground and it seems nobody wants to acknowledge it.

The cardboard cut-out of a real social worker or community nurse still hangs by a thread on the notice board, and the tissue paper patient/client has been all but obliterated by coffee spilt from the polystyrene cup that was knocked over in the dash to get to another meeting.

What is overlooked is that the carer too is not only paddling her own canoe, but has a passenger tilting and swaying the balance, making it doubly hard to stay afloat. And you thought she was disinterested and apathetic because she didn't manage to turn up to be informed of new initiatives that would change her life?
If only she believed in fairytales!
She too is coping with the rapids. No good calling Mayday - there's no one listening.

After a lifetime of finding ways to cope; of making sure my precious charge shall have access to as full a life as possible, I accept there are other points of view equally strongly held. It's all a question of perception.

From where I'm standing, this is mine.

CHAPTER TWENTY TWO

On the plus side, we have had four more years of 'I like you and me' days. Rightly or wrongly we chose not to trade the beautiful certainty of the present for a future that might never happen. Not worth the price. At least not yet. Not until the ageing process asserts itself to the point I know I can't care for her. But the guilt still is there, together with the fear I may not have acted in her best interests long term.

So we are out on a limb. Unsure, unsteady and afraid. But as I once read, 'To get to the fruit of a branch it is necessary to go out on a limb.' Maybe the ideal situation is yet within my grasp waiting for me to stretch further to discover it.

The gamble of giving up a place, especially one of the best available, was enormous, but in these past few years I've noticed the same ageing processes affect us both. As was predicted when she was born, Minty is getting old prematurely. I am no longer the young mother who was twenty-four years ahead of her, but now feel the chronological age gap narrowing.

For both of us there are signs of advancing years - hair greying, joints stiffening, a tendency to nap now and then, and a reluctance to change before change is essential. Short-term memory lapses all too often are embarrassing - at least to me. Minty doesn't notice. We are on the same declining helter-skelter, and in tandem. And that being the case there is a chance, just a chance, I shall outlive her. Maybe after all we shall die 'on the same day when we are a hundred and two!'

Not the most reliable logic to apply, but as good as depending on the changing fortunes of our state system.

With the aftermath of war still causing havoc in Iraq, I think often of all those mothers who must live either with Saddam's torture, or the repercussions of western intervention. They are hardly concerned with the years ahead, but in constant fear their children may not live to see another day. They would swap my problems a million times over to know their children had a future.

A salutary reminder that the only day of which we can be certain is today. Today my girl faces neither torture nor war. Today she is happy. We are sharing the fun, the humour that no-one else would understand; magic moments filled with impromptu speeches on a non-birthday, finding a familiar mug from the kitchen cupboard gift-wrapped simply because she wanted to give me something…. a bill tucked inside flowers from the florist, and secretive grins over the teacosy. Finding a special note under my pillow to tell me I'm the best Mum she's ever had, and hearing 'Welcome Home! I missed you so much!' when I've only been down the road to the dentist.

To those friends who are shaking their heads, yes, I accept I am burying mine in the sand, refusing to believe I won't live forever to care for her. I know I can't put it off for always and that one day we must try again.

And I shudder at the thought of starting each new dawn without:

'Love you.',
'Love you too.
'Millions and trillions?'
'Heaps more than that!'
'What shall we do today?
'Let's make it special – chicken and mushrooms for lunch?'

'Ooh yes. In the cosy pub if it rains and on our 'piazza' if the sun is shining.

And yes, we must get it right next time. The one to accustom her self to the unfamiliar, but with absolute conviction that it could really be a 'second home,' and the other to relinquish a daily experience of a wholesomeness, warmth, and generosity of spirit I

206

have yet to discover in a so called 'normal' human being. It is as if I have been privileged to glimpse that ultimate goodness of which humanity is capable.

I *will* try. But not today. Tomorrow maybe. Or perhaps the God who sent her to me will stem the ravages of physical and mental decay and keep me on my feet until the time comes to give back the precious life that was entrusted to my care.

Today we shall celebrate, put on the sunglasses, and eat cornflakes by candlelight!

SAFE AS HOUSES

Janet Wade

From scholarship girl to businesswoman, Kate Benson's story is a tumultuous one.

Her first love, Tom Heydon, whom she believes to be in the past when they each continue their careers in separate continents, permeates the novel through to its end.

Years later, returning from America with husband Duncan, Kate seeks out her cousin Jonathan, and their shared interest in design impacts on her eventual entry into the fashion world. Meanwhile from a chance meeting with Emmeline Charlesworth, she builds on the success of a market stall and embarks on a business venture that is to shape their lives.

Success seems self-perpetuating and her business extends to Paris where Armand and Marie-Jeanne Cardules enter the story.

Duncan's adultery and subsequent attempt to ruin her bring her to the brink of financial collapse. But it is Jonathan's tragic accident that finally breaks her resolve to continue the same path, and on inheriting a responsibility for her handicapped brother, she maps out a future that will encompass his needs and provide security for them both.

When this venture captures the imagination of Jonathan's two sons, Kate decides on a somewhat eccentric retirement in Paris where developments surrounding Tom occur up to the last page.

ISBN 0-9548598-1-2